I0606037

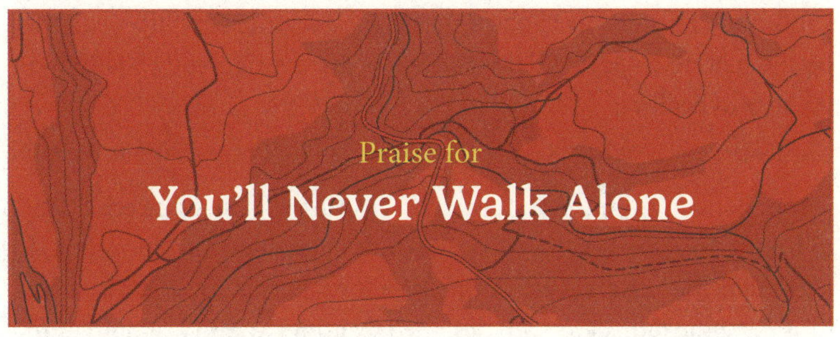

"Giese's story joyously jumped on my heart like it's a trampoline. Wise, tender, and funny as hell, this book inspires us to be better."

—**Joshua Mohr,** author, *Model Citizen*

"*You'll Never Walk Alone* offers the most memorable, restorative, stimulating experience nature has to offer, and Jo Giese is the perfect guide to waterfall medicine."

—**Dr. Wallace J. Nichols,** author, *Blue Mind*

"*You'll Never Walk Alone* is an inspirational tour de force. Beautifully written, it tells a story of overcoming adversity, surviving surgical traumas and permanent injury to walk again, hike again, enjoy the bounties of nature, and experience the full richness and beauty of life. This spectacular testament to the human spirit will lift the reader to a heightened appreciation of the power of positive thinking and the abundant possibilities for a life well lived."

—**Albert Litewka,** founding board chair and CEO, *Los Angeles Review of Books*

"This story of the medical system's failure in treating a simple injury is heartbreaking and disappointing. The author maintained her passion despite the complex route to healing she was given. A powerful read!"

—**Alexis E. Dixon,** MD, foot and ankle surgeon

"This is a remarkable story of overcoming 99.99 percent odds and experiencing a medical miracle. Jo Giese's continued pursuit of waterfalls is truly inspiring."

—**Steve Schaumberger,** author, *Sunrise to Sunset*

"This book reminds us to show up for the adventures of life—whether on the path to a spectacular waterfall or discovering body wisdom on the way to healing."

—Ann Todhunter Brode, author, *A Guide to Body Wisdom*

"From her beginnings wandering in Seward Park's Magnificent Forest, to hiking to waterfalls in New Zealand, Patagonia, and Montana, Jo Giese puts the 'waterfall effect' on paper for others to soak up its healing mist. Like the Olmsteds who designed Central Park, Jo exemplifies the restorative properties of nature in her engaging, intermittently amusing, determined, and inspiring struggle to regain the ability to hike to the waterfalls she loves."

—Paul Talbert, author, *Wild Isle in the City: Tales from Seward Park's First 100 Years*

"*You'll Never Walk Alone* is a refreshing reminder of the healing power of nature and the limitless capacity of the human spirit to challenge adversity. Jo Giese's story of resilience and recovery should help us experience our next walk in the woods as an inspiring journey."

—Robert Asahina, author, *Just Americans*

"In *You'll Never Walk Alone,* Jo Giese brings a journalist's clarity and a survivor's heart to a story that is as harrowing as it is uplifting. Her journey through injury, missteps in care, and the long road to recovery is told with honesty and courage. This book is a moving tribute to perseverance, and a beacon for anyone who's ever had to find their way back to themselves."

—Brenda Snow, author of *Diagnosed: The Essential Guide to Navigating the Patient's Journey*

"Absolutely outstanding and inspiring, *You'll Never Walk Alone* is a must-read! It masterfully reveals how nature can heal and uplift the spirit, while shining a light on the power of community and connection in overcoming life's toughest challenges. Highly recommended for anyone seeking adventure, hope, and heart!"

—Ari Block, host of the *Story Samurai* podcast

You'll Never Walk Alone

Previous Books by Jo Giese

The Good Food Compendium

A Woman's Path

Never Sit If You Can Dance: Lessons from My Mother

You'll Never Walk Alone

A Hiker's Memoir of Adventure, Tragedy, and Defying the Odds

JO GIESE

www.amplifypublishing.com

You'll Never Walk Alone: A Hiker's Memoir of Adventure, Tragedy, and Defying the Odds

The author has tried to recreate events, locales, and conversations from her memories of them. In order to maintain their anonymity, in some instances she has changed the names of individuals and places. She may have changed some identifying characteristics and details such as physical properties, occupations, and places of residence.

Oboz Local Hero photos in chapter 22 and on page 219 taken by Kenny Gamblin, Oboz Footwear.
Author photo on back dust jacket flap taken by Dana Fineman.
All other photos courtesy of the author.

For more information, please contact:
Amplify Publishing, an imprint of Amplify Publishing Group
620 Herndon Parkway, Suite 220
Herndon, VA 20170
info@amplifypublishing.com

Library of Congress Control Number: 2025912139

CPSIA Code: PRV1025A

ISBN-13: 979-8-89138-691-4

Printed in the United States

"Though your dreams be tossed and blown
Walk on, walk on, with hope in your heart
And you'll never walk alone.
You'll never walk alone."

—Lyric from "You'll Never Walk Alone,"
by Richard Rodgers and Oscar Hammerstein II

Contents

PART TWO

Prologue

There are two stories interwoven here. There's the inside story—the medical, the multiple surgeries, being stuck in bed, relying on the knee scooter. And there's the outside story—my passion for hiking to waterfalls. Waterfalls provide me with a shortcut to happiness. Call me a waterfall junkie, but if hiking is good for you, hiking to waterfalls is even better for all the reasons I'll mention.

I do not see this as an Achilles book. Instead, this is a story about what it takes to recover when you're given a grim diagnosis—it could be any disease, any gloomy prognosis—and what it takes to recover when many people don't: the grit, the determination, the stick-to-itiveness.

In *Between Two Kingdoms* Suleika Jaouad writes, "This is the story of my illness and my trek through the wilderness of survivorship. However, I don't see it as a cancer book, even though that's the particular lens of experience through which I wrote it. It's really about what it means to heal—what it actually takes to move forward when your life has been upended by some kind of rupture."*

Amen.

You could say I've been a hiker since I was five. I grew up in Seattle on Lake Washington, and it was around that gorgeous lake where stately evergreens grow down to its shoreline that I first started walking in nature, though at five years old I wouldn't have put it that way. The music of my childhood was the soothing sound of the lake gently lapping the shore. Nowadays, children glued to their devices have what's being called a "nature deficit disorder."

Not little Jo Ann.

Curly golden ringlets bouncing against my face, this young adventurer would trek to Seward Park in a pastel pinafore my mother had sewn, often carrying a stick slung hobo style over my shoulder, a snack dangling in a sack at the end. Since it was barely a block from our house, it was like our front yard. And because there weren't many children in the neighborhood, I always set off by myself. Years later I'd learn that Seward Park was designed by the Olmstead Brothers company, great American landscape architects from the same family who had created Central Park in New York City. Near the park's entrance, I'd pass the colorful rhododendrons and the masses of lily pads floating by the shoreline. Then I'd reach the swimming beach where I'd eventually take lessons from the lifeguards, with its red brick bathhouse and a concession stand that was usually closed. I'd meander over to the swing sets and take a few pumps. Then I'd leave the public playground and enter my favorite

* Suleika Jaouad, *Between Two Kingdoms* (New York: Random House Publishing Group, 2021).

private place: a walking path in the old-growth forest that led up to an amphitheater in the middle of the peninsula.

At Easter, I'd go up there extra early for the sunrise service. If I had unbuckled my Mary Janes, I could have felt the lovely soft bark on the soles of my feet. That forest path, always unpopulated, with Douglas firs and red cedars reaching two to three stories tall, was my hidden, secret, happy place, and this was a half-century before the Japanese popularized *shinrin-yoku*, "forest-bathing," defined as spending time among trees. Qing Li, author of *Forest Bathing: How Trees Can Help You Find Health and Happiness*, writes about connecting with nature through our sense of sight, hearing, taste, smell, and touch, which was exactly what little Jo Ann was doing. I wasn't knowingly doing forest therapy, and I didn't know about "healing forests," but after connecting with that childhood joy, forests and nature have been my lifelong holy, sacred landscape.

Not everyone was enthusiastic about my youthful forest activities. A retired cop, who was our next-door neighbor, cautioned my mother that she shouldn't let me do that by myself. "She likes it," Mom shrugged. My mother, the original non-helicopter parent, and little Jo Ann, the original free-range child.

You could also say I've been waterfall-centric my whole life. My parents once took me to visit a massive waterfall just east of Seattle. Snoqualmie Falls is exceptional: it's about 270 feet long and 100 feet wide. As I stood on the observation deck, tingling with the vibrations from the water thundering right in front of us, waterfalls became my "fix." Waterfalling was even a major part of my college education. For my senior thesis in American Studies, I chose "Frank Lloyd Wright's Contribution to American Architecture," and one of Wright's favorite houses, which I couldn't get enough of, was Fallingwater, the masterpiece he had built on top of a waterfall in Pennsylvania. The Fallingwater website explains that it blends humanity, nature, and architecture so that each is improved by the relationship. That captures exactly how I feel when I visit a waterfall—improved by the experience.

Part One

CHAPTER 1

Life Can Change on a Dime

I was upstairs in my office, only half-concentrating because I had an ear tuned to Lana's car arriving. It was a rare rainy November afternoon, which made our roads especially slick and treacherous, so I was concerned about Lana. She's from Croatia and hadn't started driving until she moved to the US in her thirties. As a new and nervous driver, she'd stick to the side streets, never daring to venture onto LA's high-speed freeways. Pacific Coast Highway, where dozens of people have died in car accidents, is the only way to get to our house, and probably the most dangerous road Lana had ever driven.

When the doorbell rang, it threw me off because Lana was a bit earlier than I'd expected. But I didn't want my friend to get soaking wet out there on the sidewalk, so I dropped my writing and dashed down the two flights of stairs to greet her. Although I was holding onto the banister, in my haste I missed the bottom two steps and went flying *horizontally!*

"*Shit!*" I screamed. That's my go-to blasphemy in any predicament. Years ago, when I worked as a reporter at WNBC-TV in New York, I was justifiably nervous if some upset happened and I'd be heard spewing that expletive on air.

Ed, my husband, heard the crash and came running. While I was still face down on the rug in the hallway, I asked him to let Lana in. "She's getting wet," I said, putting my hands on the floor and trying to push myself up but stumbling back.

Something was wrong, but what?

With a wet Lana on one side and Ed on the other, they lifted me up. It was instantly apparent that I could not stand on my left leg.

"Let's get you to Urgent Care," said Ed.

Urgent Care was ten miles away; the ER was twenty. Ed rushed out to the garage and found a spare pair of crutches. The crutches dug into my underarms as I hobbled a few feet to the garage door, managed the two steps down, and plopped into the back seat of Ed's car.

Lana climbed in, arms around me, warming me with her parka as Ed backed out of the garage into the dark night. As if the accident wasn't bad enough, it was also a weird night. Since Southern California gets so little rain, things can go badly wrong in a hurry. The traffic lights were out as Ed turned onto the Pacific Coast Highway, windshield wipers thwacking back and forth against the torrential rain. So few cars were splashing by in the dark, it was spooky.

With Lana on one side, Ed on the other, and rain pelting us, I crutched into our neighborhood Urgent Care just before it closed. A nurse immediately showed us down the hall and into the back room. Dripping wet, Lana's curly black hair was even curlier as she hovered next to my gurney. "If only I hadn't been outside," she said, "this wouldn't have happened."

"It wasn't your fault," I assured her.

This was November 30, 2018, pre-COVID when there was no distancing—and this was Urgent Care where there's no privacy, even when the skimpy white curtain is pulled partially closed, separating one bed from another. While I was getting my left ankle X-rayed, Lana overheard that the patient on the next examination table had just had half her face bitten off by a horse. Motioning toward the other patient, Lana whispered, "She thinks your ankle situation is worse than losing part of her face."

Pointing to a screen that backlit the X-ray of my left ankle, the doctor showed us a white line that had been my Achilles tendon. It was completely torn. Even the doctor seemed shaken. "I hate to tell you this," she said, "but it looks like you'll need surgery."

"This is not good news," Ed sighed.

The Achilles tendon is the heel cord at the back of the leg—the largest, strongest, thickest tendon in the body. It attaches the calf to the heel. The tendon was named for Achilles, the hero of the Trojan war, by the anatomist Philip Verheyen. Verheyen named the tendon in reference to a mythological account of Achilles as a baby, when his mother dipped him in the River Styx to render his body invulnerable. The heel by which she had held him had not been touched by the water, however, rendering it vulnerable, and he was eventually killed by a poison dart to that very heel.

A rupture occurs when the tendon rips completely. I'm no Trojan hero, but apparently my heel was vulnerable, too. While we were still at Urgent Care waiting for my ankle to be bandaged, I ignored the NO CELL PHONE sign and called the orthopedic surgeon we knew. Although I felt like a show-off—*Look how well-connected I am; I have the personal cell number of our doctor*—I was grateful Fred answered immediately. I'm sure I sounded frightened as I sputtered about The Accident. He said he'd see me first thing the next morning. I had always thought he had a soft spot for me because I'm a writer, and for Ed because he'd been a hot-shot DC lawyer, the brainy kind who had argued important cases at the Supreme Court.

Life can change on a dime—sometimes it's a plus, sometimes not. A doorbell rings, you race down a flight of stairs, and your life is changed forever.

At eight o'clock the next morning, we rode the elevator up to the fifth floor, and Ed wheeled me into the Orthopedic Institute of Los Angeles in the wheelchair he'd rented from Urgent Care. He figured the whole thing would be a slog, but that it'd be over in time for us to visit Montana for Christmas, and Norway for New Years to see the Northern Lights. Boy, was he wrong.

The dull, beige lobby could have used a freshening—fresh paint, fresh upholstery. It could seat a dozen or more, and it was already crowding up with ambulatory and nonambulatory, pre-op and post-op patients. It had a busy vibe like a subway platform, everyone checking their watches, anxiously anticipating their train. Here, they waited for their name to be called to see one of nine orthopedists. The receptionist, who had recognized me and smiled hello as Ed wheeled me in, was fielding multiple calls at the same time. On the far wall there was, as always, a video playing of Fred explaining orthopedic hip procedures, his specialty. The mix of crutches, canes, wheelchairs, and casts could have been depressing, but it wasn't—because many of the patients were young athletes (some with their parents), and after an orthopedic tweak here or there, they'd happily go on to play and win more games.

A nurse helped me up on the examination table. As I unbuttoned the cuff on my sleeve and rolled it back so she could take my blood pressure, I was startled. The inside of my forearm, from my elbow to my wrist and including the inside of my palm where I'd put my hands out to brace myself against the fall, were gravely bruised and had already turned purple. Even more startling was what we saw as the nurse gently unwound the Urgent Care bandages. My swollen left ankle and foot had already turned a sickly black. Ed and I exchanged a look of horror.

The doctor—let's call him Fred Eisner—was a much lauded, famous hip doctor who specialized in working with athletes, especially NBA basketball players. For half a century, I'd hiked locally, nationally, and internationally, usually to waterfalls, so that qualified me as an athlete of sorts. Hiking is part of my DNA. In winter, I had hiked to frozen waterfalls in Big Sky, Montana. In springtime, I'd slogged the marshy Gangtey Nature Trail in Bhutan. Although I'd just turned seventy at the time of my injury, I didn't look it. I probably didn't act like it, either. I was a youthful seventy. I could still do the splits and sometimes did, at dinner parties after some wine. Samantha, Fred's scheduler, usually had a fresh eight-by-ten of one of our recent hikes on her bulletin board. Today's photo was of me being dropped by helicopter into a remote location in New Zealand.

Ten months before The Accident. Through some fishing buddies, Ed had learned about a fly-fishing lodge on the South Island of New Zealand. Located outside of Wanaka on the banks of the Makarora River, the lodge had four modest rooms and one Robinson R44 helicopter. New Zealanders boasted that the lodge was located in the trophy-trout capital of the world, with a focus on heli-fishing for hardcore fishermen.

To be dropped into a totally wild, untouched area, and to fish on a river loaded with large brown and rainbow trout, miles from anywhere with no other fishermen around, seemed like a once-in-a-lifetime experience to Ed.

When Ed and I had met nine years prior, I had tried fly-fishing with him from a float boat on the Yellowstone. New girlfriends will try anything once, right? As it turned out, I wasn't an angler—I liked to float but not to fish. So, years later, I contacted the owner of the lodge in New Zealand and asked about heli-hiking. While Ed was fishing, couldn't the helicopter drop me somewhere with a guide to hike? I asked.

New Zealand is a hiker's paradise. Since it has no predators—no bears, no snakes, no poison oak, no poison ivy—hiking would be safer for once, less scary. I've had a snake phobia since I was five, when I encountered my first nasty one coiled at the base of our mailbox in Seattle. That early encounter left me with snake PTSD for life. In elementary school when there was a picture of one in a book—see, I don't even like writing the word again—I'd tape a thick piece of paper over it so I couldn't see it. Once when I was hiking in Big Sur, one slithered across the trail in front of me, and I jumped so high I landed on the back of a startled guy in front of me. "It was just a garter," someone in the hiking group said. I didn't care. Poisonous or not, big or not, I was snake-averse—and I still am. So I was relieved that in New Zealand, I'd have a reprieve from being attentive about who might be slithering by. There'd also be no rounding a bend and coming upon a bear, which is a real possibility at our place in Montana. The only thing that was harsh in New Zealand were the mosquitos, which would require face masks, and this was four years before COVID.

The lodge was so fish-centric that the owner wasn't happy about my extra request for a hiking guide. It took multiple calls where I felt like I was badgering him until he finally, reluctantly, agreed to see if he could somehow dig up a hiking guide.

After coffee the first morning, Ed packed up his fishing gear and, at six-foot-three, ducked into the little Robbie R44, whose blades were already whapping loudly on the helipad just a few dozen yards away. It was February, midsummer in New Zealand, and it was a beautiful, mild day with temperatures in the seventies, perfect weather for us and the helicopter. When a friend heard Ed was heli-fishing, he asked, "Is that when you dangle your hook and line from the plane?"

No. That's where they drop Ed and a guide near a remote river, and he gets to spend all day fishing for rainbows and browns, and he never encounters another fisherman.

When I told friends, mostly non-hikers, that I'd be heli-hiking, a response was: "That'll put you at the top of the mountain. Cool! Then you don't have to walk up. That'll be easier." Spoken like the words of a true amateur, because seasoned hikers know that walking down is harder, especially on your knees.

Dion Mathewson, the pilot at the lodge, explained about helicopters and hiking. "We don't put you in at the summit," he said. "Besides, there are no tracks [trails] up there, and the slope is mostly scree."

Ed's guide was Adam, a college graduate who was taking a gap year. After Dion deposited Ed and Adam on an isolated river, he flew back for me and Ket Hazledine, the hiking guide the lodge had found.

Preparing to go heli-hiking in New Zealand.

In the four-seater helicopter, I got to sit in the front next to the pilot, and it was like gliding in a glass globe with the most astonishing 180-degree views of the Aspiring Mountains. When Dion shot us at full speed straight through the valley with the peaks rising sharply on both sides, it was take-your-breath-away stunning.

Flying freely in such a little helicopter reminded me of flying in my dad's Seabee, a four-passenger float plane. My dad's Seattle-based company had a job repairing turbines near the Skagit River, but he couldn't get anyone to fly him in. He was told it was too dangerous, not safe to land there. So Dad and Mom went to the Midwest to pick up a Seabee and headed home on the southern route, flying visually because Dad was not instrument certified. Since no one in the family would fly with him—everyone thought he hadn't had enough instruction—I got to accompany him on flights from Seattle north to the jobsite in Skagit. There's always supposed to be someone on board who can act as a copilot and land the plane in an emergency. Dad had six-year-old me. No wonder I became an adventurer. The front windshield blew out once as we were flying over the Cascades. I described this incident to my therapist and then wondered if it had really happened. Had I imagined it? Years later, I discovered proof: a black-and-white 16 mm home movie my father had shot—yes, he was both new pilot and family filmmaker—which showed a happy six-year-old, grinning broadly, her mass of curls blowing in the windshield-less breeze against the stunning snowcapped backdrop of the Cascades.

I enjoyed my ride in the cute Robbie R44 so much. Ed said it reminded him of a VW with wings. Two years after Ed and I were in New Zealand, however, a *Los Angeles Times* article entitled "Danger

Spins from the Sky" reported that the helicopter had a terrible history. The Robinson R44, the world's best-selling civilian helicopter, had been involved in more than forty-two fatal crashes in the US between 2006 and 2016, a rate nearly 50 percent higher than the other civilian helicopters tracked by the Federal Aviation Administration.* Scores of R44 pilots and passengers had been killed in post-crash fires in helicopters that had dropped from the sky when they suddenly lost lift. In 2016, the year we were in New Zealand, their government accident investigators placed the Robinson on its "watch list" for most serious transportation safety concerns. As *The Los Angeles Times* reported, it is not a nonhazardous flying machine. It's exceptionally deadly.

After the exciting twenty-minute heli-ride, which was over way too soon for me (remember, I didn't yet know its lethal history), Ket and I were dropped into a distant valley. In New Zealand, many spectacular wild areas are only accessible by air, and with the rotor blades still thwacking, the pilot yelled that he'd be back around four o'clock, six hours later. When you're dropped into a remote wilderness with no one around, and the helicopter grows smaller and smaller as it whirls up and away, there can be a feeling of dread. What if something happens? What if the weather closes in and the pilot can't return?

That panicky feeling vanished as I was overcome by the beauty of the valley. The treeless lowland extended forever as Ket and I started tramping—tramping is what New Zealanders call hiking—away

---

* Kim Christensen and Ben Welsh, "Danger Spins from the Sky," *Los Angeles Times*, November 18, 2018. https://www.latimes.com/projects/la-me-robinson-helicopters/.

from the valley floor toward a slender waterfall in the far distance. From the air this valley had looked like a flat field with high grasses, easy walking. But what had looked like lovely golden grasses blowing softly in the wind turned out to be a swampy wetland with bad breath. Mucking through the spongy marshland required focused effort. I had to place my foot down safely where it wasn't too muddy and mushy so it wouldn't sink too far. Then I had to retrieve it *fast* so it wouldn't get stuck in the oozing muck. Every step was tricky, and this was back when I was sure-footed.

I pulled my hair into a ponytail to get it out of my eyes. This was mindful hiking at its most extreme. I couldn't have done it without the hiking poles. Out in the middle of nowhere you do not want to twist your ankle, or worse. It was slow going.

A non-hiker might ask, "You do this on purpose, for fun, and you pay to do it?"

Yes. Yes. Yes. This is my pleasure, and experiencing that first narrow waterfall with no one around was worth wading through a swampy marshland for over an hour.

Every waterfall is different. The water sounds different, falls differently, smells different, looks different. No two are alike. In Brazil at Iguazu Falls, Ed and I walked on the edge on *top* of the world's longest waterfall; in Iceland, we walked *behind* a waterfall. This first one in New Zealand wasn't a big, wide, take-your-breath-away falls. This long sliver of a quiet waterfall was barely three feet across the top where it gushed over a high rocky cliff. Since it was the low flow of late summer, there was also almost no water in the splashdown. For a special moment this was Ket's and my private waterfall, a small, hidden jewel for us to savor.

"The best is yet to come!" said Ket, a conspiratorial tone to her voice.

It was fun tramping with Ket. Her open, easy friendliness reminded me of people in Bozeman, Montana, where Ed had a house when we met. The smiles on those rural Montana folks linger, and their conversations are slower, chattier than rushed city folks. Ket, fifty-seven, a blonde dressed in a pink hiking shirt and matching sunglasses she'd pushed back on her head, was a world-class mountain climber. If waterfalls were in my blood, mountaineering was in hers. With ropes and crampons, this petite woman in pink had summitted three mountains in Nepal, two in Peru, and one in New Zealand.

After experiencing that first waterfall, we headed back and started fording Boundary Creek, which was seriously challenging. At times we were wading up to our knees in freezing mountain water so clean and fresh that Ket demonstrated it was drinkable. Crossing that cranky creek was both difficult and dangerous. The creek bed was composed of rock shards so sharp they poked up at the soles of my sturdy boots. We continued roughing it, the crunch of stones underfoot. This experience demanded that I was in the best shape of my life—and I was.

As I reveled in this remote adventure, there was no way I could have known in just a few months I wouldn't be able to take even one step on a flat surface, let alone successfully navigate such a challenging creek bed. I had no way of knowing in just a few years, if ever, that I could do something like that again.

The long hallway to Fred's suite of offices displayed an impressive collection of framed jerseys, autographed by athletes he'd operated on. He entered the examination room, dressed in a crisply starched shirt and khakis. No stiff, white coat for Fred. I was sitting on the elevated examination table, my injured ankle dangling over the side.

"Hi, *JoGiese!*" Fred always called me by both names, usually mispronouncing my last name, and running them together as if they were one.

"Hi, Fred." My late husband had been a physician, an internist, the kind of doctor who was so super-confident he didn't need to stand on formalities, didn't need to use the honorific Doctor, so I didn't either.

Fred barely glanced at any of the X-rays and hardly looked at my ankle. He explained to Ed and me that there were two approaches: "One, do nothing," he said. "But that's not for you. That's for sedentary people. Two, do surgery to reattach the tendon, and that's the approach you want." I felt I was in good hands. "I used to do Achilles surgery, twenty, thirty years ago," Fred continued. "I can do this!"

That was Friday, and he put me on his schedule for surgery first thing Monday morning.

Looking back, that was the critical moment when Ed and I should have taken a breath, thanked Fred, and left. We should've taken the time, slowly and thoroughly, to research doctors who specialized in Achilles surgery *right now,* not two or three decades before. We should have calmed down and gotten a second and a third opinion.

Since I could *not* walk, though, I was just relieved we had someone right in front of us, someone local, someone we knew. When Fred had operated on a minor tear years ago, it had turned out okay. So, when he said he could help, we jumped at the opportunity.

Let's both of us—reader and writer—pause here because there's no way to overstate how this hasty decision will forever impact my ambulatory life and cause a major life quake. Ed and I are natural optimists. We're always tipping the scales in favor of everything working out. We cling to sunshine and counting our blessings. But extreme optimism in the face of medical adversity can have its drawbacks. Viktor Frankl coined the term "tragic optimism." We can apply that here, because when it comes to our health, optimism can get us in trouble, as you'll see. Although this is ultimately a story of resilience and recovery, it's also a story of two otherwise smart people who were overly optimistic. Sometimes that's good; other times not so much.

The whole experience in New Zealand had been so refreshing, a prayer in the wilderness. Post–New Zealand, when my friend Linda saw my photos, she said, "You look like a kid. Heli-hiking must be anti-aging!"

Meanwhile, Ed had been fishing. Since he fly-fishes out of a drift boat in Montana, he was nervous and had wondered if New Zealand wade-fishing was something he couldn't do because of his artificial right ankle. He'd been afraid the ground would be too uneven—afraid he'd fall, that his ankle brace would get wet, or he'd hurt himself. Yet he did it!

Ironically, it turned out the person who would best understand the situation with my ankle was Ed. Born with a deformed right ankle and a foot that toed in, he'd had three ankle surgeries as an adult, ended up with a rare artificial ankle, and also wore a stiff black brace for stability and balance. When we were engaged, in the interest of extreme full disclosure, he took me to Baltimore to Mercy Hospital to meet Mark Meyerson, his ankle surgeon, and to see his X-ray, which clearly showed that his ankle had never been properly aligned in surgery. Think of a ball and a square that are off-center from each other by five to ten degrees. That was Ed's right ankle after surgery. Dr. Meyerson had said it would probably last him five years and he'd have to have it redone; so far, it had lasted twenty. After my Achilles debacle, we'd be a perfectly mismatched couple—Ed's right ankle and my left ankle. What are the chances of *that*?

Mid-creek in New Zealand, I picked up a shiny black stone that had a single white stripe encircling it like a halo. I showed it to Ket. "I collect these," I told her. "I call them Lucky Stones." I explained that a friend had introduced me to these gems. A confluence of geological events has to occur to produce these everyday, ordinary beauties. Millions of years ago, rock buried deep in the earth had been forced up to the surface; as the rock was pushed upward, some cracked open, and a layer of quartz had flowed into the fracture. "When these rocks erode away from young mountain ranges," I said, looking up at the peaks surrounding the valley, "the water action at a beach or alongside a river, or a creek like here, tumbles them into smooth pebbles."

In the see-through water, I spotted more. I'm picky. I told Ket that I only collect Lucky Stones with a pristine, uninterrupted white stripe going all the way around. I handed Ket a pretty one and told her what I tell my friends: "If you make a wish on it, the wish will come true." We stuffed so many in our pockets, we didn't have room for more.

We kept crisscrossing that creek, something like sixty times, and I still hadn't seen or heard the next waterfall, the big one. "I bet it doesn't exist," I teased. Ket was impossibly sure-footed, which was a good thing since she planned to climb the Matterhorn in Switzerland that summer. She smiled and kept charging ahead.

Finally, we came around a corner, and there it was! It had been hidden by a mountain ridge. On the spot, Ket called the unnamed waterfall "Spectacular!" Because it was. This second waterfall, with its powerful seventy-foot drop, had only been three kilometers away, but it had taken us four hours to reach because of the difficult creek bed.

To see such a glorious sight untouched in nature, unmarked on a map, with no one around, is a rare experience. At the very top where white water crashed down, there was a scraggle of bushes and trees. There was no viewing ledge, no protective guardrail for tourists, because there were no tourists. There were no public restrooms. There were no government signs at the edge of the turquoise glacial pond, like the ones at other hiking tracks in New Zealand. This one was off the charts. It was a magnificent secret spot, our secret spot.

Balancing on the slick, wet stones next to the river bottom, I felt the cool mist, inhaled deep breaths of the super-oxygenated cascading water, and felt myself happily filling with super-oxygenated energy. Waterfalls provide a shortcut to happiness. For me, they're magic. I could have lingered all day and returned the next for more. As a hiking buddy had once said to me, "Time we spend watching waterfalls doesn't count against our lifespan."

What's so amazing is that waterfalls can do this all day long. There's no *on* or *off* button. Depending on the season of the year, the water will fall freely and fiercely all day and all night. No rest for a waterfall.

The science to support the relaxation of being near waterfalls is well documented. According to Dr. John Seifert, a professor of exercise physiology at Montana State University, research has shown that being in nature and making a deep connection without the distractions of everyday life—*plus* the soothing, rhythmic sound of waterfalls—can lower one's heart rate and blood pressure and raise oxytocin levels. Science writer Florence Williams calls this the "Nature Fix."

Waterfalls also exude "negative air ions." Ions are particles in the air that are positively or negatively charged. Ironically, negative ions are the good ones, and they're said to offer an energizing and refreshing effect. They're particularly abundant in forests near waterfalls, rivers, and streams. The air near a waterfall can contain as many as one hundred thousand negative ions per cubic centimeter, while the air in your office might have as few as one hundred per cubic centimeter. Scientists first discovered the special air around waterfalls over a hundred years ago, and now it's considered the *waterfall effect*.

I didn't need to change my heart rate or blood pressure. I hiked to waterfalls because the cool air, the water, and the forest are so refreshing. An American program called ParkRx encourages people to use parks, and there are more than 150 park-prescription programs in the United States. People should consider visiting parks and waterfalls for healing instead of swallowing another aspirin, and more doctors should suggest "hiking to waterfalls" as a prescription.

CHAPTER 2

Being a Pedestrian

The Monday after The Accident. A smiling Fred waved at us post-op in the recovery area. Dressed in scrubs, with one of those silly-looking light-green surgical caps on his head, he told Ed and me that he'd successfully reattached the tendon. To keep it immobilized, my leg was enclosed in a soft cast from ankle to knee. He was on his way to a vacation—scuba diving in the Caribbean, I think—and said he'd see us when he returned. I was given pages of discharge instructions, which included no walking, showering, driving, or cooking.

Whether you call it walking, striding, hiking, or trekking, I'd been lucky to be a pedestrian. I'd never had a reason to be on a first-name basis with terms like "heel strike" and "load response." However, as this story unfolds, you'll see that having an intimate relationship with the biodynamics of gait will be essential to my recovery.

Aside from watching a toddler tilting and tottering as they struggle to stand up and take their first wobbly steps, most of us take our ability to ambulate—to take one step after another, to go from here to there—for granted. Think about it. There's no big secret to walking: it's free; people of all ages can do it; it doesn't require privilege or wealth or special equipment. It's as essential as eating or sleeping, and we don't practice eating or sleeping.

As Annabel Streets writes in *52 Ways to Walk*, putting one foot in front of the other, propelling ourselves forward, is the simplest and most natural of movements. It involves balance, coordination, and strength—and complexity, too, because the foot and ankle have twenty-six bones, thirty-three joints, and more than one hundred muscles.

Everyone has a slightly different gait, the pattern of how they walk. Differences in gait vary depending on a person's age, height, weight, sex, walking speed, and strength. My father, not my favorite person, nonetheless had a uniquely joyous gait in which he *bounced* with each step.

Taylor Isaacs, who you'll meet later in this story, has a doctorate in health promotion and human performance. Here's how he explained the biodynamics of what it takes to be an efficient pedestrian: "The gait cycle is a whole-body movement, including the movement of the lower limbs, upper limbs, pelvis, and spine," he said. "Lots of parts need to play nice with each other in order to be an effective walker. All the muscles and joints have to work together perfectly."

In my dining room after a Sunday lunch, Taylor said, "First, I check my posture. When someone's walking, their ear, hip, knee, and ankle should be in alignment. That's why I say walking is 'posture in motion.'"

"Walking is reflexive, propulsive, and dynamic, not mechanical," Taylor continued. "The brain sends a message through the spinal cord to the nerves. The nerves have to excite the muscles. The muscles contract and pull on the joint. Now if there's an injury, the body will go into what's called protective guarding. So, for example, if my Achilles tendon was ruptured, my brain would not allow me to further injure that joint. Think of your brain as being the orchestra conductor, and all your muscles and joints are members of the orchestra," Taylor explained. "That's what I mean when I say walking is very reflexive, propulsive, and dynamic. We move with our brain, and the language of the body is feel. How do we *feel*."

Walking across the room, Taylor demonstrated the essence of the gait cycle. "One gait cycle looks like this," he said. "Watch my right leg." He went on to explain that all locomotion starts with the propulsion of the big toe. That's where we push the toes down, creating forward movement. Then we have heel strike, foot flat, initial swing, load response. Even step length, even stride length, even step width, even stride width, quarter-inch ground clearance—lifting your toe a quarter inch to clear the ground—and symmetrical weight shift of pelvis over the femur.

Taylor went on to explain it in even more detail. Here's what he said: "The body can only produce as much force as it can stabilize. Let's say I weigh two hundred pounds. If I'm on my right leg, that leg is supporting two hundred pounds, and then I transfer two hundred pounds to my left leg. But if I've got a left ankle that doesn't work properly, how the hell am I supposed to bear two hundred pounds on that left leg? When I met you, Jo, you had an injured left leg and you were hopping around on one leg. Walking is putting one foot in front of another to keep yourself from falling. The opposite arm assists balance by swinging forward at the same time as the opposite leg."

These are the checkpoints: look at the person's posture, their arm position, and their leg position. Taylor calls it PAL—posture, arm position, and leg position. As the person is stepping off with his right leg, his left arm is swinging forward. "The big idea here," said Taylor, "is to have a continuous motion pattern."

CHAPTER 3

Scooter Girl

Post-op with my left leg in a cast and relying on a knee scooter to get around, I didn't have any motion pattern, continuous or otherwise. I also wasn't able to join Roya, my morning walking companion. Roya knew how much I loved her special saffron rice with *tahdig*, crispy crust topped with sweet and sour *zereshk* berries. But you can't ask your closest Persian friend to cook this favorite dish because it's too complicated. It's entirely a gift of love.

The first afternoon after my surgery, I was napping when to my surprise, Roya came upstairs, kissed me, and snuggled in bed with me, cuddling her head against my shoulder. She hugged me the way my mother would have if she'd still been alive. Roya had delivered huge pots of *tahdig* with *zereshk* berries, and curried chicken stew. It was so delicious it made me swoon. Roya joked that her saffron rice was why her husband had married her—but she hadn't made it for him in twenty years. "Then Bozy sees me making it and taking it to you!" She laughed and said Bozy was jealous. He had asked for a serving, but she told him, "No, it's all for Jo!"

Sometimes Lana stopped by after work, sat in the wheelchair next to my bed, and ate dinner with me. I was a compliant patient, unlike my sister-in-law. She had been instructed not to exert herself for four to six weeks after surgery, but insisted four days was her limit. Four days after surgery she went to the gym. I wasn't heading to the gym, but I did get restless lying upstairs in bed, staring at the ceiling, so I happened to be downstairs when Noelle, another neighbor, came over with a baking sheet of her tasty roasted chicken with faro, and a warm apple cake. Noelle's food was enough to last us for days, but the most memorable part was sitting in the window seat in the kitchen with my leg elevated, Noelle next to me, holding my hand. Noelle and I had never held hands before, but a medical ordeal often demands a new closeness—from the patient and the patient's friends.

Frank Bruni, who has written about losing his eyesight, says, "It's important to realize that no matter what your illness is, you're not a patient twenty-four hours a day. Much of your day is still pleasant. The sun still shines, you spend time with friends, food still tastes good. All these things are just as enjoyable as before."*

Such a scary ordeal can break down barriers, cut through formalities, and create a new sense of intimacy. Adversity can bring friends closer. That's the part that heals. Although we live in a community that boasts a glitzy reputation associated with celebrities, sunshine, beaches, and bikinis, my Malibu is different. My Malibu is about hiking in the Santa Monica Mountains and "hiking" Zuma Beach. Our neighborhood doesn't have a drop-in reputation, but friends

---

* Frank Bruni, *The Beauty of Dusk: On Vision Lost and Found* (New York: Simon & Schuster, 2022).

dropping in—bringing food and flowers, but mostly bringing themselves—was the healing part. Another friend, who self-describes as a Jewish grandmother, because she is, brought Ed's favorite pot roast and potatoes, comfort food for him, and Karen and Arnold stayed for dinner. I'm a social person, so I enjoy friends coming and going. When I'm healthy, I'm always staging gatherings: the Broad Beach Dinner Club, the Scrabble Club, and before I met Ed, the Hot Tub Club.

My nephew and his wife sent specialty ice cream in six quirky flavors. And flowers, there were so many beautiful flowers. Some included a note wishing me a "speedy recovery," because that's what most people can tolerate. Most people don't want a medical situation to drag on and on. They don't want to be attentive for too long, and when they ask how you're doing, they want an upbeat answer.

Three days post-op, I wore flannel pajamas and camped out downstairs in our kitchen window seat, licking a strawberry popsicle, my leg elevated on a pile of pillows. All the area rugs had been taken up because my knee scooter tripped on them. The dining room smelled flowery, mostly of roses and lilies from all the get-well bouquets. To pass the time, I chatted with the repairman as he serviced the elevator. It may sound fancy to have an elevator in one's house, but we had done it for my mother.

"My mom was called Babe," I told the repairman. "We named it Babe's Elevator." My mother, who'd always been active, said to me, "Never sit if you can dance." At ninety-five, she had started using a walker. Since we didn't have a bedroom downstairs, there was no way she could have hoisted herself upstairs.

I also explained to the serviceman that because I'm claustrophobic, I'd never ridden in it. Although years ago, I'd hung a large mirror on the back wall to make the tiny, tight space feel bigger, I'd never even stood in there. Now that I needed to use it—I suppose I could've scooted up and down the stairs on my butt, dragging my left leg in the cast—it was being serviced because I was terrified of it malfunctioning with me trapped inside.

I rode it for the first time the night of The Accident, after we returned from Urgent Care. Aware of my claustrophobia, Lana held me tight as the pine box went up. The first time I used it by myself, I rolled in on my knee scooter, pressed the button for the second floor, and *waited* and *waited* and *waited* for the accordion door to roll closed. The door clicked shut, and the long, silent pause before the motor started lasted way too long. That eternity creeped me out and gave me too much time to think. My mind whipped to the emergency instructions taped inside a cabinet in the garage. Would Ed, who is smart but not handy, be able to find them and understand how to stop the elevator and get me out? I looked down at the ALARM button and my eyes fastened on the red emergency phone. Did it work? Then the elevator started to lift upward, groaning as it made the laborious twenty-three-second ascent. When it settled on the second floor, and the accordion door finally opened, I exhaled as I scootered out quickly.

I told the technician about The Accident. "I just missed the corner of that wine cabinet," I said, my eyes widening at the thought of smashing into that.

"My previous service call wasn't so lucky," he said. "He had a similar accident, but he hit his head on the edge of a cupboard and he's a quadriplegic now."

I elevated my leg on a stack of pillows for ten days—ice on for twenty minutes, ice off for twenty minutes. Ice is nice. Ice is my friend. Feeling grungy from not bathing, I scootered in for my post-op appointment. To inject some fun into this unfun medical journey, I'd attached a silly bicycle bell to the handlebars of my scooter—*ding-a-ling*! Friends called me Scooter Girl.

Instead of the frumpy pajamas I'd been wearing, I dressed in a casual, comfortable blue outfit. The royal-blue flared pants had ample room for my cast, and I wore a blue Patagonia puffy vest and matching blue glasses. I felt optimistic and cheerful. The sutures were coming out, I could shower, and I could ditch the *temporary* scooter and begin weight-bearing and walking!

Even better, Ed would get a reprieve too. He'd no longer have to figure out how to fold the scooter, hoist it up, and somehow stuff the awkward device into the trunk, all while cursing.

In a small, quiet examination room at Fred's office, the nurse had warm hands as he gently scissored off the soft cast and began tweezing at the tiny Steri-Strips.

Fred sauntered in, looking tan and relaxed from his vacation. "Wait!" he said to the nurse. "That isn't healing."

CHAPTER 4

Scooter Girl Is Stuck Riding the Scooter

It turned out my wound had died. It was necrotic.

Necrotic.

I'm not sure I even knew the word before I heard it that moment. I'd been totally healthy, in terrific shape, with no underlying medical conditions that would have impaired the healing. I hiked weekly, worked out two to three times a week, and had been the picture of blazing, good health. Think helicopter hiking in New Zealand, not for the faint of heart. Could this big, dead, yucky area down there surrounded with tiny blisters turn into sepsis? Could the infection spread throughout my body? Had the cast been on too long? Should it have been removed earlier, before Fred returned from his vacation?

Fred mumbled something about an ice burn, that I'd kept the ice on too long, too close to the wound. So the necrosis was my fault?

"The ice burned the skin," he said.

"I don't understand," I said, confused.

It didn't make sense. The medical ice packs were so freezing cold I had wrapped them in a dishtowel for protection. Otherwise, I couldn't tolerate them. And I'd followed his instructions carefully—ice twenty minutes on, twenty minutes off.

Ed thought an ice burn was possible but unlikely. Afterward, when it was just the two of us, he said to me, "It's one thing to have a burn; it's another to have a hole. In Fred's heart of hearts, he knows that whatever happened wasn't because of an ice burn."

We'd soon learn that fluid-filled blisters around a wound are sometimes characteristic of a necrotic wound and have nothing to do with ice. Later, when another orthopedist heard the story, he shook his head. "That's typical," he said. "When something goes wrong, blame it on the patient."

I acknowledge there are far worse conditions than mine. I wasn't going blind or deaf. I didn't have Parkinsonism. I didn't have cancer. I hadn't had a stroke. I didn't have a spinal cord injury like the people I'll meet later on this journey. And what would I rather lose, my sight, my hearing, my ability to walk? As Frank Bruni wrote in *The Beauty of Dusk*, "There are circumstances infinitely more daunting that the tilt and blur and potential fade of my vision."*

For that first post-op appointment, I'd arrived jaunty and happy, all fresh, crisp and well dressed in a blue outfit. Now instead of getting a prescription for physical therapy, getting out of there, and walking again, I was absolutely devastated. I got a Controlled Ankle Motion (CAM) boot, I was stuck riding the scooter, Ed was stuck struggling to fold it up and cram it in the trunk, and I had an appointment to see a wound doctor.

---

* Bruni, *The Beauty of Dusk*.

This downward turn of events unnerved and frightened me. I don't think I'd been so scared since my encounter with a bear. When people ask how big the bear was, I give the standard Montana answer: a bear in your house is as big as a skyscraper.

CHAPTER 5

Little Bear Ranch

Seven years before The Accident. We were in Bozeman at the house Ed had before we met. One mid-July morning, we'd gone out and grabbed a quick lunch. On our return, I was walking in from the garage, my arms loaded with too many bulky shopping bags—those flimsy, slippery, plastic kind—so I was looking down, fully focused on not dropping and breaking anything, especially the bottles of wine that were about to slip out of my arms. The Bozeman house has a long, straight hallway with a mudroom on the right and a pantry on the left. The kitchen is the last destination at the very end. When I finally looked up, about seven feet from the kitchen, I found myself eye-to-eye with a black bear, standing right in front of me.

A bear!

A bear in our kitchen!

A bear standing in our kitchen!

A bear standing in our kitchen in front of me!

The bear stood with his back to the counter, his furry face staring directly at me, with nothing between us. I was face-to-face with a five-foot-tall Ursus Americanus.

I yelled, *BEAR!* as I ducked to the right into the laundry room. Ed was still in the garage. I dumped my armload on top of the dryer and slid the creaky pocket doors shut. The doors are loose, not tight-fitting. They barely meet in the center, and they don't lock. All it would take was one swipe of a bear paw, and the flimsy doors would be history, and so would I.

I took out my phone to call 911, but my fingers were trembling. Besides, I was so frightened I'd forgotten we had no cell reception up there. In a place where guns are part of the rugged Western ethos, people often ask if we have guns. Most of the neighbors on our mountain do; we do not. Besides, if we did have a gun, what were the chances we would've stored it in the laundry room?

Montana is bear country. The Bear Alert site warns that all bears are dangerous, and if you encounter a bear, do NOT make eye contact. First mistake, I'd already done that. They also advise to always carry bear spray. Of course, we carry it when we hike, but come on, we don't keep a gun or bear spray in the laundry room.

With a grizzly encounter, you're advised to lie down in a fetal position; with a black bear, you're supposed to make noise. Out on the trail, it's safest to continuously make noise, even if it's just a mumbled conversation or bear bells jangling on hiking poles to alert bears to where you are so they will stay away. Even if I'd remembered that advice, which I hadn't, if I made noise while I was stuck in the laundry room, wouldn't I be calling attention to myself and maybe inviting injury from a two-hundred-pound beast? A neighbor on our mountain had just been attacked by a moose, and he ended up with sixty stitches in his head.

"I'm going around to the front to let the bear out!" There was an urgency in Ed's voice I'd never heard. I guess he decided better about that because a few moments later he yelled, "Come to the garage and we'll go get help!"

Go to the garage?

How was I supposed to go to the garage?

I'm usually good in a crisis. Cool and calm. I don't break down, don't panic. In Southern California, I have an emergency list for important items to grab when a fire is blazing and we have mandatory evacuation orders. I had no emergency list for this predicament—a bear in the house in Montana.

This moment will remain embedded deep in my psyche as one of the most harrowing moments of my life. If I pulled the rickety pocket doors apart, would I be face-to-face with the bear again? The two windows in the laundry room were too high and too tiny to crawl out of. I couldn't help but replay a mess of stories that scared me to death. *The Bozeman Chronicle*'s sensational front-page articles about the growing bear population—471,000 black bears in the US—and the incidents between bears and humans:

"Bear Mauls Hiker"

"Bear Bites Camper"

"Bear Attacks Backcountry Guide"

What was next? "Bear Attacks Homeowner in Laundry Room"?

There was no safe exit.

Think about it. What would you have done? The bear knew where I was, but I didn't know where he was. I put my ear to one of the doors. I didn't hear anything. I was trapped, and if the doors were to give way…

I stashed the phone in my pocket and with a flood of adrenaline, trembling, I knew what I had to do. I would slide the doors apart and run for my life out to the garage.

The old doors were sticky and obstinate. What if I tried to pry them open and they didn't part enough? What if I slipped and fell when I attempted to run?

I cracked open the doors an inch or two—no bear. Could he be just around the corner, a few feet away?

The hallway is a straight line from the kitchen to the garage. I parted the doors. I ran for my life, making a beeline toward the garage, sprinting, hoping the bear wouldn't bring me down.

Ed had the engine running. Safe in his Tahoe, I was still shaking.

Just as we were leaving to seek help from the fire station at the bottom of our mountain, we spotted the bear through the large, square window in Ed's study. He had climbed on top of Ed's electronic keyboard and stood upright, full bear body in view, watching us as we drove away. (We'd later discover the deep tooth marks he'd left on the windowsill.)

"He's waving," said Ed. "He's saying, 'Look at me! Look, who's in charge now!'"

At the foot of our mountain, volunteers stood high on ladders, painting the exterior of the firehouse. We rushed out, shouting up to them, "Does anyone have experience with bears?" They were macho-cowboy types, and of course, all three guys said they knew about bears. If they didn't, they wouldn't have admitted it. A parade of pickup trucks followed us home, and as we waited in the car, the guys threw open every door and window and shooed the bear out.

Two wardens from Montana Fish, Wildlife & Parks, Brian Lloyd and Jennifer Knarr, showed up earlier than the 911 operator had predicted. The wardens were both attractive, in their mid-thirties, and wearing freshly starched uniforms plastered with official-looking badges and insignia. After asking if we were armed—they were, we weren't—we showed them where the bear had crawled in through the kitchen window, about shoulder-height off the deck.

"Bears are acrobats," said Brian. "They only look big because of all their fur, but they can squeeze into and crawl up anything."

"You can get rid of that nasty stench with Febreze," said Jennifer. The house stank of an ugly, musky, hot bear-fur smell. "Like a fermented gym bag?" asked a friend. Worse, much worse.

Before we'd gone out that morning, I'd cracked open the window above the kitchen sink for fresh air, and because I hadn't known better, I'd left it open, but only a few inches. That's how the bear got in. He was a graceful entry artist. He hadn't broken any of the glasses in the sink.

"He was probably attracted to the small square of aged Parmesan cheese I left on the counter," I said. "It had a strong smell."

The bear was also a discriminating, dainty eater—he liked the parmesan cheese and the three bagels, but not the Finn Crisps.

"Bears have an extraordinary sense of smell," said Jennifer. "About a hundred times better than humans."

The wardens walked through the house and pieced together the story. The screens had been ripped and torn off every window on the first floor. There was a pile of fresh bear scat with visible chokecherries on the floor in the dining room, a spray of sticky pee on the kitchen floor next to the dishwasher, and deep bite marks in a green leather chair. They said it looked like there was one bear.

"The good news is that the bear was not proprietary," said Jennifer. "See these deep scratches?" She pointed to the gouges in the wooden floor in our living room. "That indicates it wanted out."

"It looks like he forgot how he got in," said Brian.

The wardens walked the exterior and pronounced our place "clean." We didn't have an outdoor barbeque, bird feeders, or garbage cans that are bear attractive. Their only suggestion was to consider pruning or removing the chokecherry bushes that trellised up onto the deck, because bears love them. (You can bet all those pretty bushes were gone the next day.) Jennifer left her business card and her personal number for us to call when the bear returned.

"The bear will return?" I asked, shocked.

"Since the bear found food here, it will be back," she said.

Ed had owned the house since 1997 and had never had a bear inside. He dismissed the idea and left the room.

"What can we do to protect ourselves if it does return?" I asked, gulping, my throat drying up.

"Bang pots and pans," said Brian. "They don't like the noise."

"Pots and pans?" I said, incredulously. "That's our dinky defense against a bear?" Nonetheless, I opened a cabinet, pulled out some pots, and clanked them together. They did make a deafening, shrill racket.

About two hours had passed when I'd just started making dinner. I looked up from the stove where I have a clear view of the front door, and the bear—*our bear*—was standing outside the glass panel on the left, as if he were about to ring the doorbell. While I kept the bear in sight, I called the warden, who I now thought of as the Bear Warden. To my relief, I was not put on hold, no mediocre Muzak at a tense time like that. Jennifer said she'd dispatch a trap, and the bear would be removed and taken one hundred miles away to a new territory.

Very quickly, another warden hauled a metal cylinder trap about ten feet long onto our driveway. He baited the ramp on the trap's door with a moist line of fermented fruit.

We spent a sleepless, dark, sweltering, summer night, hyperalert for sounds that the bear had returned. If the bear had returned, lured by the fermented fruit, wouldn't we have heard the loud *bang* of the trap's door slamming shut?

We heard nothing.

By first light, I tiptoed downstairs out to the garage where a small window looked out on the cylinder. The door to the cylinder was shut! Was our bear inside? Or had something else been trapped—a coyote, a deer? I didn't know who was in there or if anyone was in there. Maybe it had accidentally snapped shut on itself.

I rushed and called the Bear Warden, and with Jennifer promising to stay on the phone, I quietly unlocked the door from the garage. Stealthily sneaking out, I cautiously approached the cylinder, keeping my distance.

That's when I saw him, trapped.

Peering meekly out through the wire mesh, the bear looked sad—smaller, pitiful.

Quickly, a transport warden arrived. "It'll be relocated in another territory," he said as he hitched the cylinder up to his truck.

At every stage, the super-quick response was impressive from the wardens at Montana's Fish, Wildlife & Parks. This transport warden paused before stepping up into his truck. "Yours is an adolescent bear, about two years old, and you're lucky. The next house I'm going to wasn't so fortunate," he said. "The homeowners in Big Sky had gone to Bozeman for dinner. The bear was trapped in their house for twelve hours. It rampaged the place, tore it to pieces."

He hauled the bear away, heading carefully down our windy driveway, passing the spot where a Little Bear Ranch sign would later be posted. After we remodeled Ed's house, turning it into our home, a friend asked what we were going to name it. We resisted. Ours is not one of those iconic Western spreads with acreage, cattle, and an archway that requires a name.

"It deserves a name!" our friend said, not letting up.

"Little Bear Ranch," Ed said on the spur of the moment.

The name is a joke. Our place isn't a ranch, and, as you know, the bear wasn't little.

CHAPTER 6

The Glass Coffin

As I've said, I'm a hiker—or I *was* a hiker—and so is Ed. Alice, the mutual friend who introduced us, wrote this in her email:

> *August 29, 2008*
>
> *What fun it would be if you two decided to have a meal or hike together sometime soon.*
>
> *Ed, Jo just returned from Finland and Big Sur, and I explained to her that you just arrived from your home in Montana. Both of you have lost a spouse, and both love the outdoors and people. You are two of the most interesting friends we know and deserve to have some fun and good company.*
>
> *Now I've made the introduction. You two take it from there.*

When Alice sent that email, I'd been widowed for four years

and had been on too many skanky, disappointing dates (including a guy with disgusting hair plugs), so I jumped on it and emailed this person named Ed. Since he'd only been widowed for fourteen months, this six-foot-three handsome male of the species played it cool and sauntered out for a leisurely breakfast before answering my message. On our second date, we hiked in the Santa Monica Mountains, and afterward as we lounged on the turquoise double-wide chaise on my deck, we decided to get married. I know that could sound fast, but we'd both had happy, successful marriages. We weren't battle-scared from ugly divorces. We didn't need time and space to recover. We didn't need months or years to figure this out. Besides, Ed was sixty-three, I was sixty, and we recognized something about ourselves in each other. In those four years since my husband had passed, Ed was the first man I'd met who mentioned marriage. He'd liked it and wanted to do it again.

"Celebrate everything!" my mother had often said.

Since Alice had introduced us on a Friday, and we had our first date on a Friday, Ed and I now pause and celebrate our good fortune every Friday. As I write this, we're up to 888 Fabulous Fridays. When Myles, a grandson, was recently visiting, he asked if we still do that Friday thing. "Yes," I said. "And when you fall in love, make sure you love that person enough that you'll want to celebrate them every week, too."

Nine months later, during our wedding ceremony on a hilltop in the Santa Monica Mountains, Alice explained why she'd introduced us. Her terms of endearment included our love of mountains and hiking. And we explained why we'd chosen each other:

I said to Ed: "I choose you because when you smile, you light up my life."

Ed said to me: "I choose you because you make me feel whole again."

Ed and me at our wedding at the Malibu Nature Preserve in the Santa Monica Mountains.

When you marry, you dive in for better or worse, hoping your marital waters swirl with more better than worse. We endured our Achilles nightmare as a team. I say "our" nightmare because when you're married and experiencing a serious medical situation, you go through it together. My recovery was still a non-recovery. I was not walking, I had an appointment with some wound doctor, and there was no positive end in sight.

When a good friend asked how my ordeal was impacting my marriage, I surprised myself by saying that tending to me was bringing out a side of Ed I'd never known. At the time of The Accident, we'd been married ten years. Before that, Ed had been a litigator with Kirkland & Ellis, a snazzy legal firm in Washington, DC. His office, adorned with multiple couches and a gorgeous Oriental rug—which was now in our living room—had overlooked the White House. He was whip smart and super competent, but now when I could not walk, could not even make my own simple breakfast of yogurt and berries and was forced to call on him all day and all night, even if I just needed a stupid tissue—"Eddie, could you do me a favor..."—he was softer, more relaxed, gentler, downright tender. It wasn't as if he hadn't been like this before, but he became more so. Ed, the caregiver, the person who cares.

Why should I have been surprised? His late wife had multiple myeloma, and when he was sixty, he had given up his law practice to take care of her for two years. They'd been married for forty-one years when she died at sixty-two.

Apparently, Ed and I share this caregiving gene. My late husband, a doctor, had visited too many patients in rehab facilities, and he'd told me he wanted no part of it for himself. So, in the last year of his life, I had set up an infirmary at home with a hospital bed in our living room. Although it was the saddest, unhappiest time, and I'd never want to go through it again, I also felt fortunate I was able to do that for him.

After the area around my Achilles turned necrotic, Fred referred me to a pal of his who he said used to do Achilles repair. From all the breast implants on display in his Beverly Hills office, it was clear this doctor's specialty was no longer Achilles. After removing the bandages, he took a quick look at the sickly area that had been my left ankle and immediately dispatched me to a colleague, a wound doctor.

A large, muscular man in a white coat called my name in the reception area. As I scootered after him, it didn't feel like a typical encounter with a nurse in a doctor's office. In the examination room, I asked him, "What's your background?"

"I was a paramedic in the US Air Force." He guided me to a reclining chair. Too quickly and too roughly, this paramilitary guy started tearing off the yards of bandages that went from my foot up to my knee.

"Hey, careful there!" I said, terrified. I couldn't stand anyone going near that delicate area, and this ex–air force guy did not have a gentle touch. "A little slower, please."

Once the bandages were off and the dressing was exposed, the nurse lifted away the slimy, moist squares of gauze that had covered the wound, and unleashed a putrid-smelling cloud into the tiny room. I winced, embarrassed that a part of me could smell that rotten. Using a device that looked like a turkey baster, he started flushing the wound. It stung.

"*Stop!*" I said.

The gruff guy spoke in military-ese. No friendly "Hi, Jo!" No smile to set me at ease. A tall man in green scrubs entered and introduced himself as Dr. Anderson. The air force guy, at attention, said, "Giese, here, sir."

As you can probably tell, I wasn't going to be on a first-name basis with this group, and I didn't care. You know how with some people you instantly click and have great chemistry? Not here. And it was mutual; they weren't trying to get to know me, either.

I was nearly horizontal in the reclining chair, my naked, disgusting-smelling ankle fully extended, when the doctor rolled up on a stool. "We're going to debride the wound," he said, still not making eye contact.

"Debride it?" I gulped.

"We'll thoroughly clean it, remove the callus," he said. "It helps the wound heal by removing the dead tissue."

The oozing wound had shriveled into a sickly black area twice the size of a half-dollar, with crusty edges. The doctor explained that the black part was a dead scab that needed to come off, as did the edges. The nurse had arranged scissors and a scalpel nearby on a tray. As the doctor reached for the surgical tweezers, I stiffened.

First, he zeroed in on a scraggly, stiff, yellowish crust poking up on the left side of the dark hole. "*Shit!*" I screamed. I bolted up, yanking my leg away. I yelled so loud that anyone out in the reception area, including Ed, could've heard me. "That hurts like hell!" I was bracing myself, gripping the edge of the chair, sweating. "It feels like you're sticking a sharp needle in there!"

"You've got to stay still," he said, frustrated. "Don't move. I can't do this if you move."

Don't move? I was incredulous. "It feels like you're going after it with a razor." I sat up. "I can't take much more of this."

After a few more futile attempts at snipping around the edges with the tiny scissors, he failed—we failed—because I could not tolerate the intense pain. He suggested that next time we should numb the area first. But wouldn't that require jabbing a sharp needle into the area?

With a fresh, clean dressing softly covering the ghastly wound, and new bandages loosely wound up to my knee, I got on my scooter and left the room as fast as I could pump with my good foot. "Come on, let's get out of here," I said to Ed, motioning toward the exit. As we waited for the elevator, I said, "That doctor has the personality of a doorknob."

"He has the worst bedside manner of anyone I've ever seen," Ed said. "He could be a prison guard. Such a drip. And when you look at his degrees, he was a podiatrist in Ohio, not a trauma wound doctor."

"He should be in a different business," I said. "The shoe repair business." We both laughed, which was a relief, and fun for a change.

After a few more weeks, the wound was still necrotic and I was still stuffed in the back seat of Ed's car with my leg extended, ice packs resting over the bandages—with the ice not touching my skin, thank you, Fred. We drove sixty-four miserable, congested LA miles to Cedars-Sinai Medical Center, and still *no* progress, and then Dr. Anderson had another idea.

"Maybe you should try a hyperbaric oxygen chamber," he said.

"What?"

"It's an experimental therapy that might speed the healing."

Since I didn't want anyone to say, "Well, if only she'd tried the hyperbaric oxygen chamber—"

I didn't know anything about hyperbaric oxygen. Do you? I'd never heard of it until Dr. Anderson suggested it. The more I researched it, the more frightened I got. The idea is to put the patient into a pressure chamber like they put scuba divers in when they get "the bends." Since immune cells require oxygen to kill bacteria, putting me under higher atmospheric pressure *could* increase the oxygen concentration in the tissue, and *might* help heal my complex wound infection. (Italics mine, because this wasn't a sure shot, either.)

For my first session, Ed drove me to UCLA. I had selected the hyperbaric chamber at UCLA because of its size: I figured an eight-person unit might be less claustrophobic.

You could say we were fortunate in that Ed was no longer litigating or teaching, so he was available for this new line of work—driving Jo to medical appointments. On that sunny day, the campus was lively with smart students who looked so young and healthy, purposefully striding to classes, their backpacks loaded with books. As we waited at a red light, many students crossed Westwood

Boulevard, and I bet they took their bipedalism for granted—step after healthy step. They would not be questioning their ability to stroll around campus on this lovely Wednesday morning in mid-December.

In front of the Medical Plaza, a modern, six-story building, a valet parking attendant helped Ed wrangle the scooter out of the trunk and unfold it. We rode the elevator, which descended so slowly it felt spooky—*down, down, down*—into the bowels of the building. Clutching onto Ed, I was nauseous, like I might vomit. As if Basement 1 wasn't deep enough, we descended to Basement 2. That plunging elevator sensation creeped me out. I eyed the black nylon bag attached to the handlebars of my scooter and wondered if I could throw up in there. Feeling queasy in that enclosed elevator and already frightened about being trapped in the even more enclosed hyperbaric chamber, I somehow managed to keep down my breakfast. When the elevator door opened to Radiation Oncology, we exited quickly, disoriented.

A bubbly receptionist with the best smile pointed us toward Hyperbaric Medicine. As I scootered away, I wondered how someone could broadcast such good cheer when they were stuck working all day in a basement below a basement, a dungeon. Upbeat, colorful paintings almost distracted from the grimness of navigating one dull institutional beige hallway after another. Finally, way in the back, tucked in the furthest corner of the sub-basement, was Hyperbaric Medicine. Ed opened the door that was as heavy as a security door to a bank vault, and for the first time, I faced my nemesis: the mini submarine.

The creepy-looking white cylinder was about twenty feet long and seven feet wide: a tiny eight-person submarine that I, a claustrophobic, had to enter for ninety minutes to try and heal the deep Achilles infection that was not healing.

Ed was offered a chair next to the cockpit, while a nurse showed me to a makeshift area with a flimsy curtain where I could change into scrubs. I, who am so claustrophobic that I don't like elevators, avoid tunnels and caves, and stop breathing in underground parking garages, was terrified. Remember, I'd only just started using our elevator for the twenty-three-second ride, and that was still a stretch. How was I supposed to endure a ninety-minute session buried inside this glass coffin?

As I stepped into the scrubs, I said to the nurse, through the curtain, "I'm really scared." My voice quaked. "I'm claustrophobic." I'd been frightened by the life-and-death situation of the bear in the house, but that was nothing compared to how I felt right now. This was a different sort of bear.

"I'll get you something," she said. Everyone who worked down there was extra polite and super kind, probably because they knew none of us wanted to be there. I emerged in blue scrubs and booties, and the nurse thoughtfully handed me a little white pill, a sedative. If I'd known how traumatic it would be, I would've asked for more.

The UCLA Hyperbaric Oxygen Chamber website explained that the body's healing process and its defenses against infection are enhanced by increasing the amount of oxygen that reaches tissues. Cells deprived of oxygen start to die. The website offered glowing examples, including a reduction in the need for lower-extremity amputation in diabetic patients, and for patients with gangrene it could speed up healing.

A Hyperbaric Medicine Technician—that's what his badge read—gathered the patients, four of us reduced to semi-nakedness in scrubs and booties. He explained what to expect. "You'll be in the capsule for 114 minutes, almost two hours—"

"But . . ." I interrupted, "I thought it was ninety minutes. Not *two hours*."

"You're right," he said. "There'll be ninety minutes total of oxygen breathing time: three thirty-minute sessions, with five minutes in between to take the hood off."

"Do you announce the times?" I asked. "Tell us how much is left?" I was close to passing out.

"No."

"No?"

He looked the four of us over, paying special attention to what we were carrying. Because of the high oxygen environment and the threat of fire, we couldn't bring in newspapers, pens, watches. I didn't know then about the forty-three-year-old physical therapist who had died inside a hyperbaric chamber when it caught on fire. (I read about that later in a July 11, 2025, *New York Times* article.)

"You first," he said, motioning to me. The three others were ambulatory. Then he pointed to my scooter. "You can't take that into the chamber."

"Bbbut—" I sputtered. "I'm never without it."

"Sorry." He shook his head.

I waved an apprehensive goodbye to Ed, and another Hyperbaric Medicine Technician placed a hood on my head. It looked like a clear plastic bucket turned upside down, and it would direct more oxygen into my face. In another last-minute panic, I waved goodbye to Ed again.

Of the four patients that morning, I was the only newbie. The others, two men and a woman, were old-timers, and more relaxed. I was momentarily cheerful: I could make new hyperbaric friends and learn from them. I was curious to find out why they were here, how long they'd been coming, and if they thought it was helpful. The journalist in me wanted to ask questions. But there was barely time to exchange names before we were ushered near the noisy capsule.

I rolled up as close as I could to the capsule's door, and when I handed my scooter to a tech, I felt extremely vulnerable. Standing on my right leg, I reached out to grab hold of both sides of the doorway, quickly reached for the handrails, did a nervous one-leg hop-hop on the slanted ramp into the capsule, and instantly plopped down on the closest bench.

The small, tight chamber had a center aisle with benches on both sides, made up impeccably with fresh sheets, blankets, and pillows—like a modest motel. Sort of. Or a tiny hospital room. It smelled metallic, like the clean, closed industrial space it was.

When the four of us were inside, another Hyperbaric Medicine Technician (there was a crowd of seven or eight of them down there) said, "Since for this session there are only four of you, there's room to lie down if you want." He pointed toward the far upper end at a screen to view a film or a TV show. Because the others already knew the drill, he said to me, "Bring in whatever you want, and we'll show it."

"Will we be in here all by ourselves?" I asked, already hyperventilating.

"A technician trained in hyperbaric medicine will always be with you in the chamber." I wondered if this person would hold my hand. (He did.)

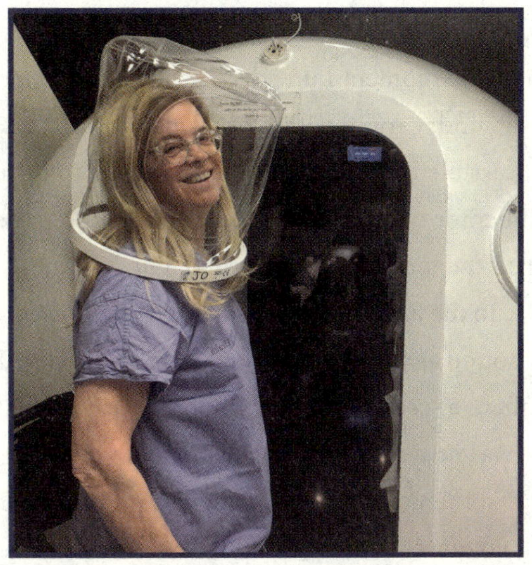

Me, about to enter the hyperbaric chamber.

We spread ourselves out, one person to a bench. A technician handed me the "legal" materials I'd brought to comfort myself—books and a stack of magazines, enough for a week or two. I made one end of my bench into a mini office, as if it would be my work area. I also had a paper cup of ice water, and the technician brought me a thin washcloth. I'd planned to dip the washcloth in the icy water and lay it across my forehead. I hadn't figured on the hood. Instead, I draped the drippy, cold cloth across my wrists.

The middle-aged man sitting across from me had already had many sessions and a dozen more to go. The other man, about the same age, seemed like an old hand at it, too. For the woman on the bench next to me, this was her last session. None of them mentioned they were there because of diabetes or being a burn victim, instances in which the hyperbaric oxygen chamber had shown some medical effectiveness.

Then came the moment I dreaded. It's one kind of terrible to be trapped in a laundry room with a bear outside; it's a totally different kind of terrible for a claustrophobic person to be locked in a closed chamber for *two hours*. The technician secured the overhead hatch, clicked the lock shut, and turned a heavy wheel to seal the capsule tight. In the first five minutes of travel time, there was a loud whooshing sound as the capsule was lowered to two to three times the atmosphere at sea level. After the pressure reached a certain point, there was no exit. What would happen if there was an earthquake? Or if someone needed to pee? (There was a bedpan.) If I freaked out, no one could rescue me because the pressure had to be released slowly, or we could get the bends, and it would kill all of us. If I were a nail-biter, I would've bitten my nails to a bloody quick.

As the submarine descended, the other woman sensed I was sick with fright. (What was the giveaway?) As the wet compress continued to drip across my wrist, she reached over and rubbed the back of my hand. Her hand was so soft, so warm, such a welcome human connection in contrast to the coldness of that monster deep-sea machine. She handed me a pink plastic barf tray, just in case.

I'd been told we could bring in a movie, but the whirring roar of the compressors was so loud it would've been a silent film.

I tried to read but could not.

I tried to meditate but could not.

I attempted deep breathing—in through my nose for three

counts, out through my mouth for five—but I gave up.

I was so sad and panicky. All I wanted was out!

To be let out!

I was traumatized, scared to death, but I also wanted to walk again, and if this could help, I had to try it.

Since we couldn't wear a watch and there was no clock in the chamber, how would we know how much more deadly time we had left? There were no windows. How could being so scared and nervous with one's adrenaline all jacked up be helpful to the healing process? Doesn't it make more sense that being calm and peaceful would be more conducive to healing? I doubted my doctors had ever been trapped inside this demonic machine. How could the technicians work all day in this underground tomb?

Later, friends chimed in. "Lucky you!" said Linda. "Hyperbaric oxygen is supposed to be good for your complexion. Spas are offering pricey hyperbaric treatments."

The only comforting aspect about this traumatic experience was that Ed was directly outside, seated next to the pilot at the cockpit, waiting for me to exit. After 114 minutes when the submarine resurfaced and the door was unlatched, this scaredy-cat was the first to hop out. Gratefully reconnected with my knee scooter and my husband, we boarded the elevator and ascended up into daylight, back to the beautiful green UCLA campus. I was on the verge of tears.

"I couldn't go through this without you," I said, clinging to Ed.

"Don't get discouraged," he said.

"They showed a documentary about Fred Rogers," I told him. "But you can't hear anything in there, and you can barely see the screen. It just gives the illusion you're being entertained." I let out a sorrowful sigh. "Maybe it's all hocus-pocus."

As I've mentioned, ironically, the person who could understand my compromised ankle the best was Ed. Because of his ankle and the fact that he needed to put on socks, lace up his brace, and wear shoes to walk, I had been the one in the family who'd jump out of bed in the mornings, turn on the gas fireplace in our bedroom, race downstairs to collect the newspapers, make the coffee, and bring it back upstairs. Now those tasks fell to Ed, too.

"How we spend our days is, of course, how we spend our lives," Annie Dillard once wrote. My days assumed a terrible rhythm: three days a week, I started at Cedars-Sinai with wound (non-) debriding, and then I was driven across town, in congested LA traffic with angry horns blaring, barely arriving at the UCLA Medical Plaza in time for my appointment in that glass coffin. The UCLA website said it takes twenty to thirty sessions to be successful. These were miserable, soul-crushing days—with nothing to show for all the energy and effort. After five days, I bailed.

"It was a big frigging waste of time and lots of torture," Ed said.

CHAPTER 7

Hearing Silence

It's an understatement to say that being trapped in that coffin didn't work for me, but what's always been restorative is to drop everything and take a hike. Any season, anywhere. A year before The Accident, Lana—yes, the same Lana who rang the doorbell that rainy night—was visiting us in Bozeman for my January birthday. After we'd enjoyed some delicious black-eyed peas for good luck in the New Year, we started the drive down the Gallatin—that gorgeous river where Brad Pitt fished in *A River Runs Through It*—except now the riverbank was mounded in cushy puffs of fluffy snow, and there were no anglers, movie star or otherwise.

It was New Year's Day, and we had the snowy road down to Ousel Falls in Big Sky almost to ourselves since it seemed most revelers were still recovering at home. Dense conifer forests glittered like snow-covered towers on both sides of the canyon.

I rolled down our windows to give us a blast of clean, cool, woodsy canyon air. Driving Ed's blue 1998 Tahoe, I was going super slow. It could get squirrely if I had to smash on the brakes too quickly in an icy patch. Once, in a white-out when snow flurries had drifted in and covered our road home in a thick white mist, it felt like I was driving inch by inch. The conditions weren't that severe on this day, but some cars had already skidded off the road into the ditch, a sad but common winter sight in Montana. The road, which had barely been plowed, was squeezed down to one lane. *Did the snow plowers have the morning off?* Although in Drivers Ed they hadn't taught us how to drive in snowy conditions, for some reason I wasn't afraid.

"I didn't know you could hike in the snow," said Lana. "It sounds like you invented this. The only hiking I've done in snow is walking to a chairlift."

"Just wait," I said, pointing up to the blue sky. The sun had just popped out between the clouds.

Unlike in summer when the parking lot at Ousel Falls is packed, every spot taken, this winter morning there was only one other car. Sparkling snow blanketed the parking lot. "I've always thought it's weird that in summer, this place is filled with families and dogs," I said. "Yet in winter, it's at its most magnificent."

While we were still inside the car, with the heater blasting, we smeared on Chapstick, and I asked Lana to hand me her boots. From the back seat, I pulled out a pair of Yaktrax. As I fought to stretch the ornery metal coils over the heel of one boot and yank it up to anchor it over the toe, I explained that Yaktrax were designed for safer winter walking. Unlike snowshoes, which are great on top of fresh, fluffy stuff, Yaktrax are for hard-packed, icy snow. "They grip securely, and the spikes bite into the snow and ice," I told Lana. "Each step will be safe and secure."

Dressed in ski pants and long underwear, we smacked squares of handwarmers against the dash to unleash their heat and stuffed them inside our gloves. We zipped up our parkas, pulled down our ski caps, and stepped cautiously onto the icy floor of the parking lot. I inhaled big gulps of the raw forest air—icy cold, crisp, and clean. "These'll help too." I grabbed a pair of hiking poles from the back and handed them to Lana.

The entry path at Ousel is narrow with a cliff-like drop-off on the downhill side. I had always thought guardrails would've been helpful, especially since it's billed as a family-friendly hike. I guess it's okay as long as the family hugs the uphill side and stays away from the steep edge. This first vertiginous section is scary, even in summer; in winter, it wouldn't be safe without Yaktrax and poles. The narrow south-facing trail was deep with snow, and someone's steps had hard-packed it, which helped. Even with the correct equipment, this steep downhill slope was an open invitation to slip and slide. One misjudged step and you could be dead. Bill Bryson, the travel writer, once described a narrow, steep, precarious trail as being like a "window ledge on a skyscraper." His description perfectly describes this entry trail, and in winter this one also had snow.

"A misstep and we'd end up down there in the ravine," said Lana. Her eyes widened as she stared down from the precipice, where we were at least a hundred feet above the valley floor. She was right. This was no place to stumble.

After a few more snowy steps, when we reached a safer area, I paused to breathe in the beauty of this dazzling winter forest. The laden tree branches were so weighted down with heavy snow that they twinkled. It was how you'd picture winter if you were a master painter. Its majesty reminded me of a line in a Mary Oliver poem: "And nothing in the forest is cute."

I was also reminded of a snowy hike Ed and I had done in Dharamshala, India. We had come up and around a curve, and right there in the middle of nowhere, in the mountainous Lower Himalayas, was a chai tea shack. I could not believe it. Surrounded by the massive Himalayas, we sat in rickety lawn chairs and sipped a civilized cup of hot tea. *Why wasn't there something this lovely back home in the Santa Monica Mountains?* I wondered. Because the bureaucracy would never allow it.

Deep in the Montana woods, down at the first curve where the forest aroma was like a Christmas tree lot, Lana whispered, "It's so quiet. I can hear the crackling of icicles in the trees. It's as if we're the only people on the planet."

There were no birds, no animals, and the bears were hibernating. We were unplugged; the only sound was our spikes crunching into the hard-packed snow.

"Everything looks the same because it's all white, so there's no depth of vision," said Lana, squinting. It was almost a white-out, and Lana was having trouble adjusting her eyes. "It's hard to know where to step when it's all the same color."

This was a side of Lana I hadn't known. Lana, a Croatian twenty-three years my junior, who had bravely escaped Sarajevo on the last plane when the Bosnian War broke out in 1992, spoke five languages. Professionally, she did soft-tissue medical massage, and she always seemed to be up for anything. Maybe I was more comfortable with this steep trail because I'd done it before, so I had an idea what to expect.

Lana and I were becoming like family. She was basically an only child. She had a brother, six years younger, who suffered from schizophrenia. He was so violent that when she visited she couldn't be in her parents' apartment alone with him, so she stayed at a nearby hotel for safety. He once pushed their mother so hard she fell on the floor, and Lana always thought that fall led to her mother's early death. It probably also led to her brother being institutionalized. After both our mothers died within a year of each other, our grief brought us closer.

Yaktraxing up another steep path, we passed a familiar bench covered in thick snow. This was the bench where our friend Arnold had collapsed one summer from altitude sickness, barely able to breathe. He could go no further. This short path—just 1.6 miles round trip—ends at an altitude of 9,370 feet, with an elevation gain of only 400 feet. But mountain life isn't for everyone. It wasn't for Arnold.

Now, after slowly navigating several slippery, icy curves, we crossed a footbridge where a friendly gurgling creek was frozen silent. Relying on our hiking poles, we made it down to the massive stone wall where noisy kids rock climb in summer and ice climb in winter, though today there were just the two of us, and not even a trickle of water flowed over the three-hundred-foot-wide wall. The free-flowing water had frozen solid on the way down and turned into a stunning turquoise icy-blue sheet a hundred feet wide.

Awe-struck, we stopped, basking in the frozen grandeur.

David Brooks has written about scattered moments of awe and wonder that wash over us unexpectedly from time to time. This was such a heavenly moment.

As I stood in front of this soulful waterfall that had been totally transformed by winter, I unconsciously put my gloved hands together in prayer. Gazing at that spectacular wall of sparkling blue ice was a sacred, spiritual, unforgettable moment. Such a feeling of astonishment makes one believe there must be a higher power. How else is it possible there's something this dazzling? Elizabeth Bernstein of *The Wall Street Journal** wrote that awe is "that emotional response to something vast that expands and challenges the way we see the world."* The stunning majesty of Ousel Falls in winter filled me with a reverential feeling of awe, a quasi-religious awe.

Time stopped as we soaked in the music of snow silence and enjoyed the absolute stillness of that forest cathedral. I felt so connected to the magic of this holy place deep in the trail. It was a prayer—being transported from everyday cares to a higher place. No distractions, no chitchat, just Nature and Winter at their very best.

Just as a waterfall's natural state is water falling, my natural state as a hiker is to be active, in motion, always up for exploring the next trail, the next adventure. That day, this waterfall was frozen in place, and there was a breathtaking majesty in its transformation. A year from then, there'd be nothing breathtakingly beautiful about this hiker frozen in place, relying on a knee scooter to get around.

---

* Elizabeth Bernstein, "Awe Makes You Feel Better. Here's a Surprising Way to Find It," *Wall Street Journal*, September 26, 2021.

Winter can transform a waterfall.

CHAPTER 8

Celebrate Everything, Especially Birthdays

Six weeks after The Accident. Somehow, we got through Christmas. The tree got decorated. Gifts got wrapped. I wrapped them sitting down. Not easy. You try it. I was worn out, still spending every day stuffed in the back seat of a car, leg elevated on pillows with ice packs, a new handicapped parking pass dangling from the rear-view mirror, being driven to appointments, even on Christmas Eve—and the appointments weren't adding up to anything.

I called Fred. "I've been conscientiously following orders, elevating and icing, and I'm getting nowhere!" I said. "And that stupid hyperbaric oxygen chamber might help some patients, but it's not doing anything but scaring me to death."

This time he referred me to a trauma wound plastic surgeon, Dr. Randy Sherman, vice chair of the surgery department and director of plastic surgery at Cedars Sinai Medical Center. I scootered in wearing a favorite red sweat suit—red is my signature color, not blood red or orange red but candy red. It boosts my spirits. I was attempting to look sparkly and upbeat, in spite of how dreadful and defeated I felt. In the waiting room, I asked the other patient, a businesswoman dressed in a dark suit, probably in her sixties, why she was there—a decidedly un-HIPAA move on my part.

"Traffic accident," she said. Brushing her short brunette hair aside, she revealed a gruesome track of black stitches across her skull. This place was clearly not plastic surgery for pretty cosmetic purposes; it was plastic surgery to repair trauma.

In an examination room, a physician's assistant named Laura Frese tenderly and slowly unwound my bandages. I turned to Ed, who was camped out in a corner of the small examination room. "Boy, she could teach that air force guy a thing or two about being gentle." Laura looked up and smiled at the compliment. Then she meticulously removed the yucky, still smelly dressing.

Dr. Sherman, a man in his sixties, was seated nearby, watching. Then cradling my naked foot in his hand, he studied the gaping black hole that had been my ankle. "The necrotic parts have to be removed," he said. "*Surgically.*" He paused to make sure I understood the seriousness of what he was suggesting. He was proposing a two-part surgery. First, he'd clean and debride the wound. Then Fred Eisner, the orthopedist, would go in and make sure the Achilles was attached.

I'd wasted a whole month with that Anderson guy digging around, manually trying to debride the wound with those nasty tweezers. This was the expert I should have been seeing all along.

"Well, if this is what I need," I sighed, "let's get it done."

I'm not a depressed kind of person. I like embracing every day, feeling upbeat, positive, joyful. But I also like walking on the beach, hiking in the mountains, driving my own car, and traveling to places I've never been. Like Norway.

I had long dreamt of seeing the Northern Lights. The aurora borealis was up there at the top of my bucket list. For New Years, we had plans to visit Tromsø, Norway, and experience the dancing waves of the green polar lights that cover the Norwegian sky. Before The Accident, I'd gotten a pair of especially warm and thick flannel pajamas for the Norwegian winter, and I'd been taking photography lessons to understand which shutter speeds would best capture the aurora borealis. I also had a new tripod to mount my new wide-angle camera so I could shoot with the super slow shutter speed that was required.

Instead, we'd had to cancel that adventure. To raise my spirits before the next surgery, Ed hosted a gathering of friends and neighbors to celebrate my January birthday. I love birthdays, mine and everyone else's. Birthdays give us an extra excuse to pause and celebrate. I love the cake, the candles, the song, the gift-wrapped presents. But more than that, it's a once-a-year chance to shine a spotlight on a special friend. Or, at the very least, send a beautiful card to someone far away. If you're my friend and you're birthday-reticent, I have to restrain my exuberance. I suppose by the time some people are in their seventies, when they turn seventy-one to be exact, they might wanna forget the whole thing. That would never have occurred to me. I am my mother's daughter—Babe's daughter—and Babe had said, "Celebrate everything, especially birthdays!"

Since Ed wasn't used to cooking for fifteen, on a Sunday

afternoon three days before my next surgery, he threw a dessert party. The cakes were displayed on our kitchen island. A large round cake with white frosting said in scratchy red letters, "Happy Birthday Joe." Another read "Get Well Joe." Must've been the same cake decorator. A smaller chocolate one read, "Never Sit If You Can Dance," the title of my upcoming book. The center of the table was decorated with a long rectangular box of white rosebuds, a gift from Ed's West Coast family. I dressed up in a sheer white blouse with gold spangles, and silvery culottes in a sparkly fabric.

The sliding glass doors to the deck were pushed wide open, welcoming soft ocean breezes. Even though it was the middle of the day, I scootered around lighting candles on the dining room table, the kitchen island, the wine cabinet. A citrusy scent mingled with the offshore breezes. Ed's piano teacher, Bond, whom I'd known for thirty years, and his husband, Bruce, were the first to arrive. Their clutch of colorful mylar Happy Birthday balloons floated up to the ceiling in the entrance hallway.

"Happy Birthday, dear Jo," said Bond, kissing and hugging me. "We've been so concerned about you."

"Let's attach the balloons to my scooter's handlebars," I said. "That'll look festive."

The dining room table had been extended to accommodate everyone, and looking around at all the friends, I felt enveloped in a positive embrace. There was Johnnie who works in IT. I joke that he's our IT department. There was Arnold who publishes our local newspaper. (He was the friend who had gotten altitude sickness when he hiked the Ousel Trail with us.) There was Samantha, a romance writer, who gifted me with a cool lap desk to use in bed after my next surgery. Erika, a Guerilla Girl artist who does outrageous feminist public art installations. Even my brother, Jimmy, had flown in from Austin.

Linda, who'd just returned to the table, had a bemused look on her face. "You know that WALK sign in your bathroom?"

"You mean the traffic sign I snagged when the city of Tacoma redid their traffic signals?"

"Yes, you could think of that as your mantra," smiled Linda.

"That's weird," I said, shaking my head. "I've displayed that sign for years and never connected it with my current predicament."

Roya, my morning walking partner who'd brought that bounty of Persian food after my first surgery, helped Ed light the sparklers on the cakes. These toppers rest in the cake, and their explosion shoots four or five feet up in the air. Not your conventional, quiet birthday candle. The first sparkler shot up so high it just missed the balloons floating above my handlebars, and for once it didn't set off the fire alarm.

Science has demonstrated that patients who go into surgery with a positive attitude and a support network have a better outcome: the patient recovers faster and has less pain. I was licking an espresso ice cream cone when the group burst into "Happy Birthday." Tears in my eyes, I looked around the table from person to person, so appreciative of their friendship. Science would say that this festive gathering with ice cream cones in six flavors was setting me up for an excellent recovery. But was science right?

CHAPTER 9

Death in the OR

Forty-nine days after The Accident, forty-four days after my first surgery, and three days after the birthday party, the surgery to debride the wound and reattach my Achilles tendon was supposed to take several hours. In less than an hour, Dr. Sherman, still in scrubs, found Ed out in the waiting room. He told him that my Achilles had died. "There's nothing to reattach," he said.

When Dr. Sherman visited me at my bedside in the dimly lit recovery area, he told me the same story. "Your Achilles died. It hadn't attached, and then it died." He held up his phone. "Want to see it?"

Even in my groggy, post-anesthesia state, I could tell from the full-color image on his phone that what was once the strongest cord in my body now looked grotesque. Like a nasty little caterpillar that had turned fetal, curled in on itself, and died in a sea of black-and-green muck.

"It's dead and slimy," he said.

They talk about life after cancer. What about life after Achilles?

"So now I need an Achilles tendon transplant?"

"First things first," said Dr. Sherman, slowing me down. "Since the wound's been cleaned, it must be covered. *Surgically*. Then you can address the Achilles."

I could *not* believe it. Now we weren't even focusing on the indispensable Achilles. I was stuck tending to the dead wound?

Ed visited me in the recovery area, drew up a chair next to my bed, and rested his chin on his hand. His look, with tears in his eyes, said it all: Here we go again. But what he said was, "We'll get through this."

At the pre-op visit before my next surgery, my third surgery, Dr. Sherman discussed donor sites from where he'd harvest skin to cover the wound: my forearm or my groin. Since I'm a writer and use my hands and arms to write and type, I wasn't keen on taking skin from my arm.

An aside. Do you notice I'm not calling Dr. Sherman by his first name, Randy? From the very beginning when we went to see him, he'd taken on the role of an important authority figure, and he also registered as our last resort. I didn't care about first names and reducing the physician-patient hierarchy. *I needed this fixed.*

Both Ed and I are impatient people. It's not our best quality. Okay, it's a bad quality we share. While we were waiting for my third surgery, this time to apply the skin graft, I observed my husband morphing into a patient individual.

Because of his packed surgery schedule, Dr. Sherman's office was choregraphing this one differently. On the day of the surgery, I was supposed to stay home until an operating room was available. Then Sherman's office would phone. Ed and I passed the morning half-heartedly—he played the piano; I played Scrabble on my iPad in bed—but we were really just listening for the phone to ring.

By the time the office finally called to tell us to arrive at Cedars-Sinai by eleven to check in for my one o'clock surgery, we barely had time to get there. Ed drove, racing us through awful LA traffic—I could not miss my surgery. Upstairs in the patient area, we *waited* and *waited* and *waited*. Ed read the morning papers, and then cracked open the book he'd brought. He wasn't antsy; he never fumed about why I wasn't being called; he never kept checking his watch. He never got up and poured himself another cup of mediocre lobby coffee. He never paced the hallways like I did, whizzing around on my scooter, ringing the *ding-a-ling* bell on the handlebars, trying to amuse myself and the other patients and families who were also waiting for their surgeries.

Finally, at 1:15, fifteen minutes after my surgery was scheduled, I was paged. An associate of Dr. Sherman's came out of the OR. "I'm sorry for the delay," he said. "Dr. Sherman had an emergency. He's still in surgery. He's been in surgery since first thing this morning." He paused. "You can have your surgery later this afternoon, at five or six. Or tomorrow."

The wind out of my sails, deflated, I slumped back on the seat of the scooter. I didn't want to be his last patient after he'd already been in surgery all day. "Even the best surgeons get tired," I said. "I'll return tomorrow."

Ed didn't protest. "But we raced to get her here on time! We've waited all day!" Instead, on our way home, we used the extra time as an opportunity to try a paella restaurant I'd spotted near the hospital. Seafood paella is a family favorite for which I'm famous and which I spend days preparing—smashing the threads of saffron in a mortar and pestle, cracking the lobster legs, shelling the shrimp, rinsing clams, sautéing scallops. It was our good luck that this small, quiet restaurant was still open even though it was well past lunch time, and we were their only customers. You take your luck where you find it. Since I wasn't finding it in surgery, maybe we could find it in paella. Exactly when I was supposed to have been under anesthesia, with skin being removed from my groin and placed over my ankle, I was gorging on my favorite food, making the most of what otherwise would have been a disappointing, dismal afternoon.

Making the best of it was a gene I'd inherited from my mother. Babe made the best of it often, especially one summer when my father's company got a job repairing turbines on the Canyon Ferry Dam outside of Helena, Montana. In that hardscrabble neck of the woods—this was definitely not your welcoming Big Sky, Montana—there was nowhere to live. Not one house, no apartments. Down a no-name dirt road, Mom found a one-bedroom, one-bath shack to rent. This was no cute Martha Stewart shack. It was the real deal. Mom scrubbed and sanitized and scoured the inside of that shack until it almost sparkled. A roughneck cowboy-looking guy who was squatting in another shack up the road wandered by and asked if she'd clean up his place. Mom shot him a look. Nowadays, if a husband were to have a three-month gig in such a dump, the wife would most likely stay behind with the children, instead of dragging everyone out to the boonies. That wasn't Babe's style. She was crazy about Dad, and where he was, she'd be. We were there to keep

Daddy company. She made the best of it and so did we.

So, when we met and Ed told me he had a place in Montana, I couldn't help but remember our sad shack down that dingy dirt road. I was thinking, *Oh, please, dear God, not Montana again*. I was relieved Ed's place was different. His was halfway up a mountain with a black-bear forest behind it. (In the future a fire would blow through, and the arborist from the insurance company would tell us that 841 trees had burned, decimating the bear habitat. And yes, that habitat is undoubtedly where our bear-in-the-house had been living and hibernating.) The main road to Ed's place was dirt, but his mountain community was civilized, with family homes. The area had miles and miles of hiking trails, some leading to waterfalls. Eventually, I took Ed to Helena to see the outpost where I'd spent my twelfth summer. Maybe I'd distorted things—maybe I'd remembered it worse than it was. Nope. A half-century later, the only "improvement" was that some of the roads had names. Ours was called Cave Gulch, which seemed about right.

Ed and me on our first hike in Montana in the Lee Metcalf Wilderness on Spanish Creek Trail.

The next morning during surgery, Dr. Sherman sliced a six-inch flap from my inner left groin and attached it over the Achilles wound. I joked to Ed, "Will my ankle have pubic hair?"

In the hushed, dimly lit recovery area, Dr. Sherman said, "No exercise! No movement to tear the wound area." He spoke like an artist, fiercely protecting his latest work.

I was discharged from the hospital in a wheelchair (again) with my ankle leashed to a wound vac, a weird, clunky device that 24/7 sucks bacteria from the wound into a cylinder to remove excess mucus and promote healing in acute wounds. Since I was eager to do something to keep in shape so I wouldn't totally go to pot, in bed I started lifting weights with my upper body. It wasn't much—it wasn't the joy of trekking up a mountain—but lifting the barbells was something, and it involved no lower body movement. I spent most of the time with my leg elevated (again), and now I was also leashed to the dreaded wound vac.

I'd never met anyone who had recovered without an Achilles. There was no Achilles Foundation, no Achilles Support Group. (Ironically, there is a group called Achilles International, a nonprofit that enables people with special needs to participate in mainstream running events. In spite of its name, it has nothing to do with the Achilles tendon.) If I'd had someone to talk to who had no Achilles, that might have helped. It might have been encouraging. Or not. In a letter to the editor in *The New York Times*, Jerry Dawson described having lost his Achilles due to a postoperative infection. His story hit home. Jerry was also in his early seventies, and when he and I finally spoke, I wasn't encouraged; I was horrified. A cyclist who used to ride fifty miles a day, Jerry's Achilles had ruptured on a bike ride, and seven weeks after his first surgery, the area had become infected. The doctor who had done his surgery had been fired from the hospital in Florida for incompetence. (The Los Angeles hospital should have done the same with Fred.) When Jerry and I spoke, it was ten months after his accident, his ankle was still infected, and he was waiting to see if he needed another surgery to get rid of the infection. From his desultory tone, he sounded like he'd already thrown in the towel, had totally given up, and had no energy left to pour into more surgeries and walking again. This was not the upbeat, encouraging conversation I needed.

It's no real estate agent's exaggeration to say that the ocean view from our house is what caused my late husband and me to buy it after seeing it for only seventeen seconds. The master bedroom has an unobstructed view of the Pacific Ocean, Zuma Beach, and Point Dume, a peninsula that juts out into the sea. I looked on a map once and the immense ocean in front of our house goes uninterrupted all the way to Patagonia, almost six thousand miles. I love the powerful roaring song of the waves cresting and crashing into the shore, the kelpy, seaweedy smell, and we always enjoy counting the number of surfers in front. Or "sitters" as Ed calls them because many are amateurs just sitting out there on their boards. My favorite are extreme low tide days when the ocean has receded so far that the sand is hard-packed, and we "hike" on the beach. I especially like the drama of dark winter days when there are whitecaps and the Pacific Ocean looks more like the angry North Sea. Having grown up in Seattle, water is in my DNA, my comfort zone. But anything can get old, tiresome, monotonous. And it had. I was fed up staring out the window. What's also weird is that all those hours, days, and weeks stranded in bed, gazing out, I had no sexual longing. That was so unlike me. Is it that when one part of the body is in recovery, other parts shut down?

Restless, I was more than ready to be out of bed, unplugged from the wound vac, and enjoying a different view.

Once when we'd been traveling in Chilean Patagonia, a view played a trick on us. The Explora Lodge is located on its own waterfall, Salto Chico Falls. When we checked in, the view from the lobby was cloudy, closed-in, dismal. The famous Lake Pehoé could've been a dirty puddle in Detroit.

"We've traveled all the way to the end of the earth, Chilean Antarctica, for this?" I complained to another guest in the lobby.

"¡Espera, ya veras!" said the guest who was checking out. "When the clouds lift, you'll see."

We dumped our stuff in our room just as the moody clouds were miraculously disappearing, and the 9,843-foot snowcapped mountain range popped into view with a perfect mirror image shimmering in the now-turquoise Lake Pehoé. This transformation unfolded right in front of us. A more breathtaking welcome would be hard to imagine.

The view was so irresistible, we immediately laced up our boots and grabbed our poles and raincoats. On the hillside above the lodge, we sloshed through tall, soggy grasses and beamed like two exuberantly happy, wet kids.

Welcome to Lake Pehoé, Chile.

Post-op I couldn't do any of that—couldn't travel, couldn't hike—and I was fed up with our wonderful view. I wasn't marching over hills with a stiff breeze blowing in my hair. I wasn't trekking to Hyalite, a favorite waterfall outside of Bozeman. My endless days stuck in bed sucked. At least I wasn't like my angry sister-in-law who was so mad when she got a cancer diagnosis that she raged, asking *why me?* Why did she get cancer when she'd done everything right—ate the right foods, maintained the right weight, exercised regularly? I never felt sorry for myself that way. I thought all that negativity was a waste of energy and would get her nowhere.

In *The Beauty of Dusk: On Vision Lost and Found*, Frank Bruni writes that disability can enhance ability. He says blind people often report better hearing, that deaf people experience better vision. I understood his point, but I wasn't buying it for myself. Since I couldn't walk, could I hear or see or smell or taste better? Nope. But I did need to calm down and chill out. Since medications and alcohol don't mix, this wasn't a moment for more Ambien and chardonnay. Instead, I turned to an old standby: meditation.

I asked Maricris, the home healthcare worker who had arrived to change the dressing, to close the bedroom door when she left. Reclining in bed, I pressed play on an ancient Jack Kornfield guided meditation tape. I shut my eyes and tried to breathe—slowly breathe in for three seconds, hold it for three seconds, breathe out for five—to be still, and invite a sense of calm. This was what I'd also tried to do in the glass coffin. It hadn't worked then and it wasn't working now.

Let's put this in perspective. As I've said, what I was suffering from wasn't the worst thing in the world. I wasn't dying from heart disease and I didn't have Stage 4 pelvic cancer. I could not walk, and for a walker that felt deadly. Dr. Sherif R. Zaki, acclaimed detective of infectious disease, died at sixty-five. In his obituary his wife, Nadia Zaki, said he died in a hospital from complications of injuries sustained in a fall down a flight of steps at home. Dr. Zaki's obituary hit too close to home.

For my birthday, a friend gave me a sweatshirt with "All Good Days" written across the front. I wore it as Maricris changed the dressing again, but it was not Happy Hour.

CHAPTER 10

One of the Most Remote Places in the World

Many of us have bucket lists of places we dream of traveling to one day. You already know I'd been yearning to see the Northern Lights in Norway, and that dream got squashed by my Achilles debacle. When I was a child, "travel" had meant a road trip with my father driving his Studebaker, my mother in charge of flipping the pages in the AAA TripTik maps (this was the 1950s before GPS and Waze), with my brother and me fighting in the back seat. Because of how blessed my life had become, I'd been able to dream bigger about more exotic and far-flung destinations than accumulating miles in the family car. Ed and I had also acquired lots of frequent-flyer miles.

Five years before The Accident. We had plans to leave for the end of the earth, Chilean Patagonia. But first we had to spend a small, quiet Christmas with Babe, my ninety-seven-year-old mom; Ellen, her companion-caregiver; Jimmy, my big brother; and Lynn, his wife, in mom's apartment in a senior living community in Houston. I say "had to" reluctantly because that makes it sound like this

Christmas with Mom loomed like an unwanted obligation. I didn't feel that way, but I was excited about getting back to Chile.

This would be Mom's second-to-last Christmas, but we didn't know that then. What we did know was that we wanted to make it festive. This could sound like an oxymoron, celebrating a fun Christmas Eve in an apartment in a high-rise senior community.

Since some senior living situations have a justifiably bad reputation of being dingy and drab, filled with residents who are too old and too dull, some readers might be skeptical that it was possible to pull off a cheerful holiday vibe in Mom's apartment. Even Atul Gawande, the surgeon and author of *Being Mortal* who has written extensively about medicine and what matters in the end, expressed surprise that his dad had blossomed in a senior community. Babe blossomed, too.

It was only natural that I wanted to make Christmas extra festive for Mom since she and Dad were the ones who had introduced me to this holiday with so much enthusiasm. When I was about five and my brother six, one Christmas Eve we were at our aunt Evie and uncle Howard's house. As the sky darkened, the phone rang (prearranged), and our parents breathlessly said, "Hurry home! Santa Claus is here!" As our uncle drove, my brother and I kept looking through the treetops, searching the night sky for Santa's sleigh. As we ran into the house, Dad pointed to the sooty footprints on the carpet. "You just missed him!"

"Mrs. Claus was here too!" said Mom.

So, it's no wonder I wanted to make Christmas special for this person who had always made it wonderful for us. We weren't a conventionally religious family. I'd been an angel once in a Methodist Christmas pageant, I had a pretty pink rosary to use at mass with my Catholic childhood friend Elizabeth Drew, and after a wrenching divorce, I tried Buddhism. Christmas for us meant sharing food and gifts and goodies. I crammed pots of bright crimson poinsettias on the narrow ledge of Mom's balcony that was fourteen stories up and, unfortunately, looked down on the 610 Interstate. At this stage of her life, Babe was hard of hearing, so the idea had been that the freeway buzz wouldn't bother her so much. She'd never had any debilitating diseases, but she did suffer from peripheral neuropathy, which made her unsteady on her feet, and explained why her walker was always nearby.

Her apartment smelled fresh and piney from the brightly decorated live Christmas tree that twinkled in her living room. As I set the table for Christmas Eve dinner, I pulled out the tablecloth Mom had embroidered years before. Her largest and longest embroidery project, this gorgeous tablecloth was big enough for a wedding. "Banquet size," she said. "It's a pretty thing, isn't it?" Mom was among a legion of unsung women embroiders of her generation, and her masterpiece, which we saved for special occasions, boasted hundreds of embroidered flowers, each with a pale blue, perfectly executed French knot in its center. On the sideboard, crystal candle holders held tall, white candles that glowed behind vintage black-and-white photos of my brother and myself visiting Santa Claus, a prized collection Mom pulled out and displayed every Christmas. Jimmy, my big brother, referred to as big because he is (he's six-foot-eight and a year older than me), did a heroic job of somehow roasting a large turkey in the apartment's tiny oven.

While the apartment filled with the anticipatory aroma of the turkey roasting, and Perry Como crooned about a "White

Christmas," Babe sat, like on a throne, in her oversized, upholstered chair next to the glowing tree, happily sipping her first of two scotch-and-sodas. She was wearing a holiday orange caftan, and her thick strawberry blonde hair had been freshly styled by Able, who ran the salon down on the second floor in the building.

I'm not eager to admit this, but at times during this Christmas, there was this niggling thought that I was in a hurry for it to be over so we could start spending big, rambunctious Christmases with Ed's family and the six grandchildren. After Christmas dinner, snuggling in bed at a nearby chain hotel, I asked Ed, "Why are you okay forfeiting Christmas with your sons and grandchildren?"

"Fair is fair," he said. "I think you're doing the right thing by your mother, and I'm part of the process."

What Ed remembers most vividly about our visit was the night we took Mom and her caregiver to dinner at McCormick & Schmick's, where we scored a window table on the second floor with a primo view of all the bright Christmas lights in the shopping center below. After dinner, our plan was to drive around and see the spectacular holiday lights in River Oaks. There's this yearly tradition where ultrarich Texans compete to have their megamansions decorated more extravagantly than their neighbors. With "A Holly Jolly Christmas" playing on the radio, Ed in the passenger seat, Mom and Ellen in the back, I drove down River Oaks Boulevard. Suddenly, I spied a street that looked like it had the best, must-see, over-the-top displays, including artificial snow falling! From the far left lane, I made a sharp turn, cutting directly in front of the traffic to the right of us. Was I so dazzled by all the regal homes dressed in bling that I forgot basic driving skills? Ed says he and my mom exchanged a look: *What* is she doing? Thanks to some holiday magic, I crashed into no one and no one crashed into us; my three startled passengers were stunned into silence, as was I. We screeched to a stop in front of the most amazing mansion, where a gigantic oak tree dripped in moss had a million lights twinkling. That's when Ed, raising an eyebrow, said, "You've got to pay attention. Your mom and I were scared to death."

Can I add another River Oaks Christmas story, which I'm still not proud of? One Christmas when my brother and I were in high school, he drove us in his beat-up VW Bug to this same swanky River Oaks area. We boldly walked up the long walkways and brazenly rang the doorbells on these huge, colonial mansions, the kind I wished we lived in instead of our little rental on the other side of the tracks. This was at a time when people still opened their doors, and when they did, my brother and I said we were collecting money to feed poor children at Christmas. We had a small, brown paper bag for donations, and no official papers to identify the group we were collecting for. I don't remember how many houses we went to—just a handful—and when we figured we had enough, we hopped back into the VW Bug and scampered away with the loot. Still in the fancy part of town, we treated ourselves to the best holiday steak dinner, the kind we could not have afforded. I guess you could say we were feeding poor children.

After surviving my River Oaks driving and our otherwise lovely family Christmas, Ed and I were ready for our next adventure. Since many of Ed's fishing guides in Montana spend their winters guiding in Patagonia, he was curious about going there. One summer I'd lived in Santiago, Chile, as part of a University of Texas–University of Chile Student Leader exchange program. I'd longed to see more of the country than just Santiago and Viña Del Mar, but as a college sophomore, I had only two hundred dollars cash to last the entire summer.

Although Ed and I would arrive at the end of their summer, we'd been told to expect volatile and violent weather with wind gusts of 75 mph and higher. In Bruce Chatwin's *In Patagonia*, every other sentence describes the wind—the wind whistled, the wind-flattened garden, the wind whirring, the windswept desert, the wind blew the smell of rain, the roofs of the houses clattered in the wind. Since the focus of our Chilean adventure would be hiking, I packed our windbreakers, raincoats, plus puffy parkas.

After twenty-four solid hours of traveling, LA–Miami–Santiago–Punta Arenas, we finally landed at the tiny airstrip in Puerto Natales. Catching his first glimpse of the Andes, Ed said, "This looks like Montana with water."

"It smells like Montana, too," I said. After being stuck in questionably clean airports and stuffy airplanes, inhaling that first blast of crisp, cool evergreen mountain air was a refreshing gift.

We were driven to a hundred-year-old sheep station that had been transformed into a gem of a hotel, where on our arrival we were served a pisco sour, the national drink of Chile. The first sweet, cool sip brought back so many memories of when I'd traveled to Chile the summer after my sophomore year at UT Austin.

I'd been selected as one of eleven students to represent the

University of Texas in Chile. *The Houston Chronicle* reported that the program was designed to foster better international relations. The idea was that the student leaders of today would be the national leaders of tomorrow. Before Santiago our group was flown to Washington, DC, for briefings with legislators, ambassadors, and Latin American affairs experts. "In Washington, we'll find out how the government stands," I was quoted as saying. "We are not committed to represent this view, but it might make answering some of the questions easier." In the newspaper interview, I said I was anticipating questions on American policy in Vietnam, intervention, and the racial situation. It made me sound like a hot-shot policy wonk, much more serious than I felt. No offense, feminists, but I wouldn't have minded if the reporter had also asked what I'd be wearing. I would've described the light-blue suit I'd sewn from a Simplicity pattern. (My Home Economics sewing skills weren't up to a fancy Vogue pattern.) We toured the White House (where I wore my homemade suit) and got to visit the Oval Office, which was so much smaller than I expected.

Of the eleven students, there was the token Black, the token SDS student, and the token Blonde. How was it that the token Blonde, with limited Spanish, also became the translator for the group? One of my favorite phrases in Spanish was (and still is) *yo tengo ganas de* . . . . It has no exact translation but more or less means *I have enthusiasm for* . . . . The problem with using that catchy phrase is that it instantly branded me as a more fluent speaker than I was—I'd only had high school Spanish and two years in college—and then native speakers would be off and I'd be lost.

A memorable highlight was meeting Pablo Neruda. In a school

auditorium that was drafty, dark, and drab, all eleven of us were seated in the first row, and Pablo Neruda, who would be awarded the Nobel Prize in Literature four years later, was onstage directly in front of us, barely ten feet away. Frumpy, wearing a tired sweater, he slumped in a chair like an old uncle. I don't recall the poems he recited to us, but I remember how his profound love for his native Chilean homeland sang out in his work. That evening I became a lifelong Pablo Neruda fan, especially of his sensual love poems.

All night, I have slept with you
Next to the sea, on the island.
Wild and sweet you were between pleasure and sleep,
Between fire and water.

There's no way to overstate what a big, fat deal that trip was. First, on a campus with over forty thousand students, I was one of eleven selected. And I'd never traveled abroad. I got my first passport and landed on foreign soil for the first time. When I disembarked (in my homemade suit) and walked down the steps from the plane at the airport in Santiago, I had actually expected I would be new, different, changed—*foreign*. Hmmm, I was still the same old me.

For Ed's and my first Chilean hike in Bernardo Higgins National Park, we went out in the hotel's small motorboat. This evergreen landscape resembled the gorgeous San Juans in my hometown of Seattle, but the San Juans don't have the extra punch of frozen blue glaciers like in

Esperanza Sound. Everything here is ratchetted up several degrees, and made more intense by how remote it is and how few people venture this far to the very southernmost tip of South America.

"What's that?" I asked the guide who was piloting our boat. I was pointing at the most glorious, huge, wide, icy-blue waterfall.

He said it was a frozen glacier cascading between two mountain ranges.

After he docked our boat at a small pier, we briefly hiked, still wearing our lifejackets, through a lush evergreen forest. We exited at a dramatic spot where the Serrano Glacier, called a hanging glacier because it's "hanging" between two mountains, was shedding huge chunks of turquoise ice, which were floating on a green lake. Cool breezes blew off the glacier.

"This is exciting!" said Ed. "This is the first glacier I've seen. Except for the dwindling and dying glaciers in Glacier National Park."

"But this looks nothing like that," I said, dazzled by its beauty. "This is healthy and robust!"

Next, we were driven in a raging rainstorm across southern Patagonia toward Parque Nacional Torres del Paine. The message from the team at the Explora Lodge explained that our car trip would take about two hours and would lead us to one of the most remote places in the world.

In late afternoon, the guests—about a dozen hardy souls—gathered at the bar. A guide said, "You're here at Explora to explore, and different explorations will be offered every day."

Another guide explained how their system worked. "Every night before dinner, you'll meet with the guides." She motioned to the five or six other guides lounging around, mostly youngish college students. "You'll spend a few minutes with each guide who will try to sell you on signing up for the hike they're leading the next day. Some hikes are extreme, all-day hikes; others are half-day, more leisurely."

It was clear that if you weren't interested in hardcore hiking, this was not the place for you. A framed quote hung above the bar:

Serrano Glacier, Chilean Patagonia

"We shall not cease from exploration and the end of all our exploring will be to arrive where we started and know the place for the first time."
—T. S. Eliot

Our small bedroom had a unique feature I've never seen elsewhere, and hope to never see again. The bathroom had a window, so when you're sitting on the toilet you can look out into the bedroom. And someone in the room can look in and see you. Whose weird idea was that? The best feature in our tight, modest room was a windowsill just wide enough so we could line up our sodden, wet boots and socks to dry.

A disappointing aspect of travel, especially rigorous adventure travel, that's rarely mentioned is that you can probably expect to have less sex. The dreamy ads in glossy travel magazines suggest otherwise, especially bridal magazines touting exotic honeymoon destinations with saucy pictures. You can practically smell the promise of sex on those pages. But between jet lag and our days fully scheduled with interesting new activities in exotic new places, meeting intriguing new people, and not wanting to miss out on anything—combined with vigorous exercise—an erotic tryst can get short shrift. And on car trips, forget it. You're usually exhausted by the time you finally pull up to your destination.

When I was younger, I just knew that sex in a new place would be different. Hotel sex in Paris! I could hardly wait. (But remember, I'd also thought I'd be different when I stepped on foreign soil.) I discovered sex is sex, and an exotic location doesn't make much difference, and that's not such a bad thing, either.

On the Aoniken Mountain hike, our group consisted of us and three couples from New York City. We passed llamas and guanacos close enough to touch. Because of Montana, Ed and I are used to extreme mountain hiking, but while ascending a steep granite trail, one woman panicked and froze, clinging to the uphill side of the mountain. She was so scared that she could not go up and she could not go down. She was stuck. Clinging to the mountain.

Since the guide didn't want to disappoint the rest of us, he asked her to sit and he'd return. Once we got to the top, the summit was so quiet. *Where was all the windy commotion Bruce Chatwin had written about?*

On the Aoniken Mountain hike in Patagonia with my husband, Ed.

Our guide, reluctantly and without enthusiasm, left the group and went back to rescue the stranded woman. That's when this middle-aged woman, in questionable shape, admitted she'd never hiked. Why in the world had this New York City sidewalk-walker put herself in such a risky situation? And what was this non-hiker doing at the rugged Explora Lodge when she would've been better off at some Ritz Carlton in Palm Beach?

Our final hike was the exact opposite of the mountain hike the day before. Wearing raincoats just in case, we strolled along the super-green, mossy Rio Pingo streambed, which ended at a gentle, soft waterfall. As we'd headed by motorboat to Rio Pingo, we saw the most gorgeous iceberg, six or seven stories high with an open arch in the middle that was so large our boat could have motored through.

Iceberg, Rio Pingo, Chilean Patagonia

In *Blue Mind*, Wallace J. Nichols writes that studies by Nik Sawe of Stanford University on the brain show that in some people, the sight of inspiring natural landscapes triggers the same reward circuitry as food, sex, and money. That's me on waterfalls, even just this soft, gentle one.

"How's it possible every day gets better?" I said to Ed.

From the first glimpse of hard-to-access Patagonia from the air—the blue glacier lakes—and the first navigation in Puerto Natales, every day in Patagonia exceeded our expectations.

At a time of profound climate disruption, the landscape of Southern Chile is still a hopeful place. Maybe in the future, the big hanging glacier will be reduced to a paltry small glacier (if that), and that will feel brutal. But in spite of global warming and dire predictions about the world changing in unrecognizable ways, it's no exaggeration to say that Chilean Patagonia is still one of the most beautiful places on the planet.

CHAPTER 11

Like a Bride Being Escorted Down the Aisle

One hundred and fourteen days after The Accident. Forty-six days after the third surgery, I was back at Dr. Sherman's for a follow-up visit. The examination room felt tight and cramped: my scooter was parked in the corner, I was in the examination chair again with PA Laura Frese, and Dr. Sherman and Ed squeezed in, as well. The bandages had been removed, and the skin graft was beige and wrinkly with creepy, crinkly dried scabs along the edges.

"It looks healthy," said Dr. Sherman.

"It might be healthy, but it looks—"

"Put your left foot down," he said. When I hesitated, he said, "Put weight on it."

"Put my whole weight on it?" I raised myself up on my elbows from the reclining chair so I could hear him better. "You mean *stand on* it?" I had no confidence my injured foot would hold me. "Won't I wobble and topple over?"

I was tempted to resist because common knowledge is that you cannot stand with no Achilles, and mine had died—I did not have one. But trusting this doctor, I tentatively swung both feet over the side of the chair. Hanging onto the chair, I stood on my stable foot, maintained eye contact with Dr. Sherman, and reluctantly put my injured foot down. My naked left foot—heel and five toes—made intimate contact with a floor, a cold linoleum floor, for the first time since this medical journey had begun four months earlier. Dr. Sherman opened the door to the outside hall and motioned for me to pass through. I was incredulous. I thought I was coming in for a post-op wound check; I had no idea this would turn into a walking session.

Clinging to Ed on my left and grabbing onto Dr. Sherman's crisp white coat on my right, the three of us left the room. Later, Ed would say he'd thought I could do it, but he wasn't sure. Barefoot, I took a tentative step down the linoleum hallway, sniffling and crying, crying good tears.

For the first time I thought I saw the beginning of the end. Both men at my sides were over six feet tall, and I felt like a bride being escorted down the aisle. Or the hallway. That short first walk, being able to ambulate again, felt that important, that profound. Nurses and assistants came out to cheer me on. "You can do it! You can do it!" Everyone wanted to witness this patient starting to walk again, no longer stuck on her scooter. Time slowed as I took about ten hesitant steps and then gently turned and headed back, still holding tight to Ed and Dr. Sherman. One hundred and fourteen days immobilized, and I had taken my first twenty steps.

CHAPTER 12

Your Being Here Is Heroic

I say I felt bridal as I took those important first steps, escorted down the "aisle" at the medical center by Ed and Dr. Sherman. There are "aisles" in medical centers and "aisles" on mountain tops. When Ed and I married in 2009, our aisle was a dirt path on a rugged mountaintop at a nature preserve in the Santa Monica Mountains. When sixty-four-year-old Ed walked down the aisle, his processional music was, appropriately, "When I'm Sixty-Four," and our guests laughed. And when our guests realized that the ninety-five-year-old mother of the bride would walk the bride down the aisle, everyone clapped. I wore a red bridal gown with a train that a friend said fluttered in the breeze like a flame.

There's nothing about our wedding we didn't like. It started with a proposal on my birthday in Varanasi, India, considered by Hindus to be the spiritual center of the world. (It wasn't a total surprise; we'd already chosen the ring.) The first evening, both of us wore garlands of marigolds. A soulful flower in India, this saffron-colored blossom symbolizes strength and new beginnings. Perfect for us. We celebrated by taking an evening cruise in a traditional wooden rowboat on the Ganges. The Ganges, the Mother Ganges, is so revered that once in their lifetime every Indian must make a sacred pilgrimage to bathe in its waters to purify themselves. On our visit, the thick green-brown water looked and smelled like sludge. I told our guide I couldn't believe people were dunking themselves in such muck. "Does he look scared?" our guide asked, motioning to a young man who was wading waist-deep, smiling. Different strokes for different folks, I guess.

Our twenty-foot rowboat stood out, because in honor of our engagement our guide had outdone himself: the benches, which ran down both sides of the boat, were decorated in shocking pink cloths, and hundreds of marigold blossoms lined the length of the boat. After our boatman rowed us away from shore, he and his young assistant—she couldn't have been more than twelve—kept lighting and dropping candles into the Ganges until a long parade of lights floated behind us, a public announcement that something special was happening.

One hundred and fifty-one days after The Accident, the first week in May, Ed and I flew to Austin to attend something else that was special: a family wedding. I made my way through LAX being pushed in a wheelchair. Previously, if I'd been waiting for a flight, I'd be the one doing exercise laps around the terminal. Now I was in a wheelchair, waiting for early boarding.

I was nervous about my cousin's wedding because I was barely walking. I was still elevating and icing.

Learning to walk again wasn't my only job. I also had a job of a different sort—the launch of my joyous book *Never Sit If You Can Dance*. First, I recorded the audiobook, and that was fun because I got to dust off my skills from working in radio as a special correspondent at Marketplace. The sound engineer jiggered the mic and the script stand so I could sit in the recording studio. By the time we recorded the last chapter, in which my mother died, we were both crying.

Because my book was launching at the same time as my cousin's nuptials, I appeared on a local CBS TV show the morning of the wedding. A viewer could have seen me on *We Are Austin* in my red author suit and reached the wrong conclusion. I was only able to do that live in-studio appearance because I could sit and talk. I could manage that: sitting and talking.

From our hotel room, I did a radio interview that was broadcast from Tennessee, and the host introduced me as a bestselling author. After we were off the air, I corrected him. "No, no," he said. "Your book is already a bestseller." I checked Amazon and he was right. At least something was going well.

It was supposed to be an outdoor wedding in the late afternoon, except it started raining in the morning and never stopped. The weather could have cast a pall on everything. Instead, the rain-drenched landscape popped with fresh green life.

I wasn't popping with fresh life and it showed. Usually, I'm photogenic. I can't help it; it's hard to take a bad photo of me. Some people can high-jump or are good with numbers. I'm neither of those, but I am photogenic. Once I had a friend who wouldn't appear in pictures with me because she said I photographed too well and she didn't. I even look okay in mug shots for my driver's license and passport. Some of my best photos are when I'm glowing near a waterfall. In pictures from that wedding in Austin, I was *not* glowing. It wasn't about aesthetics. I was worn out and it showed. It took every bit of energy to leave home, travel, and navigate unfamiliar places where I didn't know how many steps I'd have to take. The pain and discomfort and worry showed. If I used to photograph fresh and robust, now I looked pale and sickly. I was still in recovery.

The morning after the wedding was the start of the Pecan Street Festival in downtown Austin, exactly the kind of corny festival I love. I enjoy poking around booths that sell old stuff: vintage tablecloths, pottery, tchotchkes. I like the relaxed weekend vibe of smiling people licking cones of pink cotton candy, enjoying sugar cookies in the shape of Texas, and chomping on roasted turkey legs. I even like the icky sweet smell of Kettle Korn swirling in those huge, hot vats. That morning, one of the nation's largest fairs was right outside the front steps of our hotel. It was irresistible. Immediately after breakfast, I kissed Eddie goodbye and set off in high spirits to scout all the good stuff.

At the first booth the vendors, mother and son hippies dressed in tie-dyed shirts, were arranging neat rows of their leather products. "Hi, how are you?" the mother said to me. She had a big friendly smile, the kind that encourages customers to look and linger. "How can I help?" she asked.

"I'm just looking," I said. I glanced at their handmade leather wares—wallets, belts, keychains—then I saw a lawn chair tucked in the shady back corner of their booth. "Would it be okay if I sat in your chair for a moment?"

"Sure, help yourself," she said as she organized bills in a cashbox, getting ready for the weekend crowd, which the local paper said was expected to be three hundred thousand.

In the back of their tent, I sank into the lawn chair and realized that was what I needed. Not a leather bracelet, barrette, or belt. *I needed to get off my foot.* I hid out in that shady, dark corner and watched the mother-son vendors stepping back, turning their heads this way and that, appraising and rearranging how their wares would look from a customer's point of view. I liked that a mother and her adult son got along so well that they could work together in such a friendly, easy way. I did not like that I had wilted after visiting the first booth.

Since I didn't want to spend my only morning at the fair stuck in that dark corner, I thanked them for their chair and set off, intending to explore the north side of the fair, a colorful maze of hundreds of tents. After managing a few more weary steps, I asked another vendor, who was selling vintage Western shirts, "How far does this go?"

"Ten blocks."

Ten blocks. Then another ten blocks back.

Usually, a fair that large would be thrilling, all the more

opportunity to meet people and see all their interesting stuff, except it turns out that morning I was not interested in looking at pipes and bongs, T-shirts, amateur ceramics, some of it arts and crap. I'd miscalculated. It was much harder than I'd expected. After barely glancing at two or three more booths, I stopped at the ice cream truck, not because I wanted a Drumstick first thing in the morning but because they had a picnic bench.

Collapsed on that bench, licking that dumb Drumstick while nearby a young guy softly strummed a banjo, I glanced down the length of the fair. The ten blocks loomed like ten miles. What was I thinking? How in the world could I have thought I was ready for this? I threw away the Drumstick and—step by impossible step—dragged myself back to the hotel discouraged and disappointed, my brain screaming: *I cannot walk!*

Ed, who had just returned from working out across the street at Gold's Gym, was in bed, reading the papers, enjoying his coffee. I was sweating and out of breath as I opened the door to our hotel room. I screamed to the walls, to the ceiling, to Ed: "*I cannot walk! I cannot walk!*"

I'm not the screaming type. In the eleven years we'd been together, I'm pretty certain he'd never heard me scream like that. "I barely managed to check out a couple booths. I could not go one step further!"

"The truth is," Ed said, "your being here is heroic."

I appreciated him saying that, but I was mad. "I'm fed up with amateur hour!" I shouted. "Getting junior college care! Dealing with all these doctors who've never treated anyone who has no Achilles!" I pulled out my phone. "I've had it! I'm leaving messages for those doctors that they must refer me to someone who has experience dealing with a patient who has no Achilles. No more amateurs!"

"This trip was premature," said Ed.

The non-walking fiasco at the street fair was a turning point that would fuel the next phase of my journey. Trapped in amateur hour, anger would be my motivator as I scrambled to find a new direction.

I'd been sad but now I was mad. It's been said that girls and women get sad; boys and men get mad. Now this one-Achillied woman was badass mad.

After the non-walking debacle at the wedding in Austin, Dr. Sherman, the trauma wound plastic surgeon who had done two of my surgeries—debriding the wound and attaching the skin flap—said it sounded like I needed gait training. But the gait guru he knew had just died. Lord, it felt like I couldn't catch a break. Instead, I started physical therapy.

I'd started PT once before, but now I had an appointment at another facility, the Sports Performance Lab in West Los Angeles, and I liked that Susan Fu, the director, was young, maybe mid-thirties, and in excellent shape. She was her own best advertisement for good health and good fitness. She listened to my story, and hesitated. "I've been in physical therapy for twelve years, and I've never seen your situation. It's extremely rare." She watched me walk across the room in my new HOKA sneakers with the roller sole. "You favor your right side," she said.

"I know." I sighed, already weary. "I can walk a few blocks and then I have to sit down. I spend a lot of time elevating and icing, and that's the only time I feel okay." Watching as Susan entered copious notes on her laptop, I added, "I might be a candidate for an Achilles tendon transplant, but I'm trying to avoid that because it's another surgery."

She motioned me to a therapy table and asked me to remove my shoes and socks. "Take off the bandage too." Reluctantly I removed the sticky edges of the bandage. "Touch your ankle. Massage it."

"Yuck!" I cringed. "I've never touched it. It grosses me out."

Pink and pruned, my wound already looked wrinkled and old. I refused to look at it or touch it. When Eleanor Henderson was researching her husband's painful and ugly skin lesions in *Everything I Have Is Yours,* she wrote about not wanting to look at them: "…it is best to hold your head as far from the screen as possible, which depending on the length of your arm is approximately three feet. If possible, close one eye. Squeeze the other one shut until you almost can't see out of it."*

To do the home exercises, I had to keep my eyes open while I massaged the left heel and skin graft for five minutes, three times a day. Susan wrote: "Don't attach any negative feelings to it. You need to train the brain to recognize it like the other side again. We got this, Jo!"

I emailed her: Since you haven't rehabbed someone with no Achilles, would it be possible to do some research? I don't want to burden you, but if we had some idea of what might have worked in a similar situation, that could be helpful.

---

* Elizabeth Henderson, *Everything I Have Is Yours* (New York: Flatiron Books, 2021).

It also would have been helpful if I knew someone who had no Achilles so I could have chatted with them and found out how they were doing. An Achilles support group. That camaraderie could have lifted my spirits, but that Jerry Dawson guy, the one person I'd spoken to who had lost his Achilles, his story was too disappointing.

Susan wrote that she was researching it. I also sent her a picture of the waterfall at Hyalite in Montana. "This is the waterfall I wanna be able to hike to," I wrote. "It's one mile in, one mile out, a gentle stroll."

Two years before The Accident, Brad, my hiking buddy, had introduced me to a new waterfall. Ed and I had connected with Brad at a gym in Bozeman. He has a BA in sports medicine from Montana State University, and when the gym closed, he branched out: he started hiking with clients in summer and skiing with them in winter. One of Brad's clients, an ob-gyn whose clinic had been the target of anti-abortion protests, recovered one summer by doing "a peak a week" with Brad. To locals, that means summitting a different mountain each week, and Brad had done that after his avalanche accident. On off days, even in his mid-sixties, he thinks nothing of doing a fifty-mile bike ride.

An iconic mountain man, and single, Brad lives a life that might be the envy of people attracted to the Mountain West—skiing and hiking and biking—and everything else is secondary, except for the two beers at happy hour every afternoon. He's a maniac athlete, and I say that affectionately. About his avalanche accident: He was skiing off-trail in the back country with friends and suddenly gravity released a sliding layer from a rushing avalanche. A five-hundred-pound chunk hit Brad and trapped him against a tree. He survived only because he wasn't skiing alone. His friend saw the accident and a chopper airlifted him out.

He said his soft-tissue injury—a complete tear of his right quadriceps—was far worse and much harder to heal from than if he'd broken a bone. After the quadricep was reattached, his doctor said to this skier, who was now crippled on crutches, "You probably won't ski again." Insensitive proclamations by professionals can be crazy-making, and Brad wasn't immune to his negative prognosis. "Every day I couldn't bear weight," he said, "and my big, strong leg shrank to nothing, and I had doubts I'd walk or ski again."

As my story unfolds, you'll see that if anyone was my athletic North Star for recovery, it was Brad. After two years of rehab, strength training, and diligence, he was able to ski again. "Most people with such an accident at fifty-one wouldn't have been able to," Brad said.

I'd only known Brad after his accident. He was always so thoughtful, empathetic, and kind as a hiking buddy. Over the years I'd met his mom, and I respected that when Lorraine needed extra attention at the senior community where she lived, Brad would drop everything and set off to help her, in spite of being nervous that his beat-up 2005 Subaru Outback would break down on the fifteen-hundred-mile round trip from Bozeman, Montana, to Mesa, Arizona.

Ed and I have a deal: when he goes fly-fishing, I go hiking with Brad. One day Brad and I were heading out on the Interstate in my SUV to Big Timber Falls.

"Look, Jo," he said, "the Crazies!"

Brad was pointing north, toward the majestic snowcapped Crazy Mountains, which dominated the horizon. "See that pointed peak with the snow? That's Crazy Peak, the highest in the range. I've been to the top—skiing, hiking, climbing," he said. "And see all the snow on the Crazies? That's a good sign for the waterfall."

This was wide-open country with nothing but pastureland, and we were bumping along on the rough National Forest dirt road that runs next to the gurgling Big Timber Creek. As we bounced along, Brad swerved to avoid the worst potholes. "We'll inch our way up," he said. "There's no traffic, so there's no reason to rush." He drove two-handed, attempting to outmaneuver the rugged road.

I rolled down our windows, and the pine-scented air smelled fresh and green. Finally, we arrived at the grassy parking lot in a picnic area. "Look," said Brad, pointing overhead. "We just happen to be at Halfmoon Campground when the half-moon is out! How cool is that?"

We geared up. Mine was your standard Patagonia-REI khaki hiking clothes. Brad dressed formidably, more like a Swiss mountaineer about to scale the Alps rather than a Montana hiking guide in August. He'd arrived to pick me up wearing khaki shorts, a black zippered jacket, and black socks that were probably support hose since the full strength in his right leg had never returned after his avalanche accident. In the picnic parking lot, he tugged a sweatband onto his forehead and pulled a black woolen ski cap over the top of it. He looked goofy. Around his chest, he'd double-cinched a seriously huge and heavy backpack. My hiking buddy was proudly overdressed for our little adventure.

Usually when you're out in nature, you're hiking *to* a waterfall—the falls are the destination, the reward, the big treat. You earned it! This time, as we pulled into the modest parking lot at Halfmoon Trail, we could already hear the roar of water. The sign at the trailhead indicated an eighth of a mile—a couple hundred steps—to the falls. Unbelievable. I'd visited one other waterfall that was this accessible. In North Carolina, you can see Looking Glass Falls from the parking lot in the Pisgah National Forest.

At Halfmoon Trail, I ambled happily through the soft grasses and swatted a thicket of shrubs out of the way to catch a first glimpse of the tons of water splitting through the narrow rock canyon, thundering down from Blue Lake, five miles up the trail.

"I would say we've nailed it," said Brad with a smile in his voice. "There's no one here except us!"

This is a textbook example of how a properly long—two-hundred-foot—dramatic waterfall should look. Nothing dainty or quiet about this one. I unhooked my fanny pack and climbed up on my hands and knees, scrambling across the flat rock ledge. Since the best place to see these falls was the edge, I called back to Brad that I was going to the rim. With a rush of endorphins, I scooted on my butt, inch by careful inch, crouching low, moving slowly over to the edge. I wanted the whole experience—the feeling of the mist on my face—so I scooched over to the brink.

Perched at edge of the waterfall in the Crazies in Montana.

"Careful there, Jo, that's an eighty-foot drop," called Brad, safely watching from the trail.

Trying not to lean too far forward, I dared to peer all the way into the splashdown. I balanced at the vertical edge, both hands splayed flat against the ledge, as if that could do any good. It's not like there were handholds to grab onto. Perched way out there with my legs dangling over the side was frightening and exhilarating. Like the time Lana and I had extra carefully Yaktraxed that icy, vertiginous trail on New Years Day, this was not a moment to choke and lose one's nerve. I could only do it because I don't suffer from a fear of heights or vertigo, and I had a pretty good sense of balance. (I say "had" because after my Achilles rupture, much of that reliable sense of balance—*pfft!*—would be gone.) The big payback for scaring myself was getting to be that up close and personal to such an astonishing waterfall. I craved that kind of experience. You know how every summer you read how someone dies at the Lower Falls in Yellowstone National Park because they want to get just a little closer to snap a better photo? My actions might sound like that of a thrill seeker, but I wasn't being that foolhardy or stupid.

The first summer after The Accident, I started PT again, this time in Bozeman. After working together for a month, Carol, the therapist, asked me to walk across the room, about fifty feet. She stood off to the side, arms crossed, studying my gait while I self-consciously tried to do my very best. Then she had me walk between the parallel bars, not touching the bars. I trusted Carol because a few years before she'd helped me recover from a meniscus tear repair on my left knee. Her mother and mine had died about the same time, and we'd commiserated together. I got a kick out of the stories about her newly widowed father, his cattle ranch near the Crazies in Big Timber, and his escapades as he started dating in his seventies. I also admired how Carol, a single woman, was purchasing her own home in town.

In a private room, Carol pointed to my hiking boots. "You're so happy with them, but they aren't helping you walk. They're keeping your foot immobilized." The physical therapist in LA had said the same thing about my boots, which felt so stable and safe.

Carol also said, "I hate to be a Debbie Downer, but you're going to be compromised for the rest of your life."

I'm going to be compromised for the rest of my life.

What gave her the right to say that? By any chance, was she related to Brad's doctor who told him after his avalanche accident that Brad, a skier, would probably never ski again? Hope is a powerful tool for healing. One of the worst things you can do is to rob someone of hope, and that was exactly what Carol was doing. Usually Carol had a packed schedule, seeing eight patients a day. Did her lack of bedside manner kill their hopes for recovery, too? Thich Nhat Hanh, with whom I'd done walking meditation in the rice paddies of North Vietnam, said, "Hope is important because it can make the present moment less difficult to bear. If we believe that tomorrow will be better, we can bear a hardship today."

When I told a local friend, who was familiar with that PT facility, about Carol's comment, she was incensed. "For someone in that position to tell you that is unacceptable!" Karie Dreyer said. "She was completely out of line. Her place is to encourage because you never know . . ." her voice drifted off. Then Karie, a horsewoman, told me the story of Vito.

"I had a horse once—a Dutch Warmblood," she said. "When Vito was about three, he impaled his shoulder on a wooden post. The nerve damage also paralyzed his leg. He wasn't able to lift it, only drag it. Through rehab and bodywork, he regained about 97 percent of his leg strength and use. Two years later, Vito was doing better, and we attended a clinic led by this famous German vet. This vet looked at Vito and said to me…" Karie paused. Years later it was still hard to tell this story. "This famous vet said, 'Why are you bothering with this horse? This horse is finished. *Kaput!* Put him to sleep. *Kaput!*' That's what he said. *Kaput!* It made me want to prove him wrong." Vito went on to become a competitive upper-level dressage horse and jumper. At the age of twenty, Vito is still sound. "I never considered him lame, just different." Looking me directly in the eye, Karie added, "Anything is possible. Shame on Carol."

Another medical professional said, "That's damaging mentally. Because in medicine, there's never a *never* and never an *always*. You look at the possibility. That person was baptized in lemon juice."

When Chris Snow, a hockey executive with the Calgary Flames of the National Hockey League, was diagnosed with amyotrophic lateral sclerosis (ALS), a progressive neurogenerative disease from which he would die at age forty-two, his wife, Kelsie Snow, felt desperate—utterly desperate—to hold onto hope, completely terrified of someone taking it away or diminishing it even a little. Because hope, it turns out, is everything.

Carol's cruel comment stung, but I was not shattered because I refused to believe her. I did not feel hopeless. I kept thinking this was something I could conquer with enough push-ups—metaphorical push-ups. She said I was kidding myself. But perhaps her negative appraisal also spurred me to redouble my determination. I would investigate everything. Maybe I needed an Achilles tendon transplant?

The trickiest part of the hike in the Crazies with Brad—and remember, this was two years before The Accident—was not activating my risk-taking muscle by perching on the rim of the falls and looking over the edge. Like in New Zealand where I hiked Boundary Creek to Spectacular Falls, and that rocky mess of a trail had been almost impassable, the trail to the next waterfall was dangerous. This extra-wide trail, about ten feet across, was composed entirely of sharp rocks.

Brad explained that the Crazies are volcanic, so the rocks are rugged and sharp. "You have to be alert," he said. "*Hyper*-alert." He said this had been an old mining trail for horse-drawn wagons.

"It doesn't look like a wagon could've made it over this," I said, trying to negotiate, step by super-precise step, over the sharp granite fins that stuck straight up like knives.

"That was before trucks and ATVs. That's why you have those hiking boots, so you won't sprain your ankle."

Upstream, we passed two young men who were wading and swimming in the freezing cold, glacial waters. They might as well have been dousing themselves in ice cubes. We made it to a wooden pedestrian bridge that had been newly constructed over the next falls. This waterfall was the polar opposite of the first—this one was low and wide, about thirty feet across, gushing gently.

The sun had popped out and for snack time, Brad stripped down to a sleeveless T-shirt that matched the green of the forest, and donned a floppy sun hat. On the lowest horizontal rail on the bridge, like the best host, he carefully lined up eight tiny, colorful Tupperware containers: chunks of cheese, apple slices, fresh cherries, grapes, cashews, carrot sticks, crackers.

We relaxed on the bridge, lounging in the sunshine. I bit into a square of cheddar cheese on a slice of apple. Snacking deep in the forest transformed that cube of ordinary grocery store cheese into something else. Taking another bite, I felt like I'd never tasted anything so fine. I was amused when I read in Shelby Stanger's *Will to Wild* that it's "almost universally acknowledged by outdoorsy people that food just tastes better outside in nature after a long hike."* Right.

I was in no rush to leave. Brad took some photos of me; I took some of him. He checked the time. He said we'd arrived at 9:30, and we should head out now at 11:00 before it got too hot.

"I'm surprised," I said. "It seemed like ten minutes."

Such a perfect day reminded me of a quote by one of my heroes, Frank Lloyd Wright, who also had a thing about waterfalls: "I believe in God, only I spell it Nature."

---

* Shelby Stanger, *Will to Wild: Adventures Great and Small to Change Your Life* (New York: Simon & Schuster, 2023).

CHAPTER 13

A Life-Threatening Event

Back in California, I was suddenly peering over another kind of precarious ledge—a life-and-death one. One afternoon, I glanced down at my abdomen. Then, to be sure, I stood sideways, half-naked in front of a full-length mirror. My abdomen was as huge as someone pregnant. Where had *that* come from?

I knew this weird new situation, whatever it was, was related to the stress and strain my body continued to experience due to the death of my Achilles, which had been throwing me off-kilter. This time, it threw me into a grave situation.

Now I know this could sound like what does this have to do with that? *Let's skip this and get back to the Achilles*, you might be thinking. But the human body is a complex, interconnected, integrated organism—and mine was rebelling against the assaulting and re-assaulting of my ankle. Nothing gets injured separately and nothing heals separately, so when the ankle necrosis compromised my immune system, it impacted my entire body. Jane Brody visited this idea in her "Personal Health" column for *The New York Times:* "The human body doesn't function in silos," she wrote. "Rather it works as an integrated whole, and what goes awry in one part of the body can affect several others."*

As I stood, still semi-naked in front of the mirror, I nervously phoned my internist, Jonathan. In a frightened voice, I said I looked like I was four or five months pregnant. Jonathan ordered me to get to the ER. Immediately. By ambulance.

While I lay scared and confused on a gurney in the hectic hallway of the ER at Providence Saint John's Hospital, Ed's warm hand holding my cold hand, an abdominal surgeon, Tracey Childs, explained that the scan revealed a severe abdominal blockage. She said I needed surgery as soon as possible, and I had to be admitted to the hospital immediately. Without emergency treatment, my complete bowel obstruction was life-threatening.

In those frantic first moments, scared to death, I blurted out, "How in the hell did I get this?"

Tracey shook her head. That moment of intense medical urgency wasn't the time to go there. Instead she said, "From this moment on, you cannot eat anything."

Fortunately, there was a room available. Upstairs in bed, stripped of my everyday clothes and wearing one of those skimpy blue hospital gowns that tie in the back, I was given the strictest instructions: I was only allowed to chew on small ice cubes and swallow the tiniest sips of water from a miniature paper cup. *Nothing by mouth* was boldly posted above my bed.

---

* Jane E. Brody, "How Vision Loss Can Affect the Brain," *New York Times*, September 7, 2021.

"How long do I have to do this?" I asked a nurse, as she handed me a tiny container of ice.

"Until your bowels are completely clear and you're ready for surgery," she said, pointing to the bathroom across from the bed, about ten steps away.

"How long does that take?" Ed asked.

"We'll see," the nurse said, hanging my chart next to the door.

As Ed headed home to pick up his essentials—clothes, razor, laptop—I asked the nurse to please get a small bed moved into the room for my husband. When Ed had his knee surgery a few years ago, I'd had a small bed in his room. There was no way Big E, as his grandchildren called him, could be expected to sleep in that fake-leather reclining chair to the left of my bed. There was also no way I was going to stay in the hospital by myself. Even in the best of circumstances, I don't like being alone. So in a hospital, with a brand-new, scary, life-threatening diagnosis, there was no way I was going to be left stranded, all by myself. Ed was too attentive to have left me alone anyway.

An aside: A few years later, Ed would be diagnosed with a serious medical condition, and I would drive him to this same hospital every day for his treatment, for twenty-eight days. It would never have occurred to me to let him go alone. Jo for Ed; Ed for Jo. We were, and are, a team. Teamwork works.

What upset me the most was that just as I was starting to make some progress walking with my non-Achillied ankle, that progress had screeched to a halt as I was hospitalized, bed-ridden, chomping on ice.

At least with my Achilles, I now sort of knew what to expect, but with this new abdominal complication, I was slammed completely off-guard, left in the dark. As I grew hungrier, my stomach growling loudly, there was no way I could have known that I'd have to keep laying in that bed, chomping on those tiny bits of ice for six long days. There was also no way I could've known I'd be discharged eight days later with seven inches of my colon removed, a fresh line of stitches across my belly, and a twenty-four-hour antibiotic drip.

Sweet Lady Jane, a popular dessert shop, is just a few blocks from Providence Saint John's Hospital. Since Ed has a sweet tooth, especially for chocolate, he'd leave for a few minutes while one of the nurses looked after me and saunter over to treat himself to a brownie, a chocolate macaroon, a chocolate chip cookie. I was happy for him getting a little pleasure; after all, he'd jettisoned everything to be by my side 24/7.

But I also said to him, "Don't you dare bring anything back here." I grew more famished by the day, by the hour, and at that stage, I didn't know how many more non-eating days were left. I couldn't stand seeing or smelling something delicious from that fabulous pastry shop.

Most of those six pre-op days were a blur, but what wasn't a blur were the friends who dropped everything to visit. Their kind visits reminded me of a passage from *A Kingdom of Tender Colors* by Seth Greenland. Diagnosed with an aggressive form of lymphatic cancer, he wrote, "Only presence has meaning. You remember who was there."*

Lana visited, and my writer friends Linda and Diane stopped

---

* Seth Greenland, *A Kingdom of Tender Colors: A Memoir of Comedy, Survival, and Love* (New York: Europa Editions, 2020).

by. I deeply appreciated their efforts. I know how awkward it can be to visit someone in the hospital. What do you say? What do you bring? How long do you stay? You don't want to be too cloying, or too piteous, and you also don't want to tire the patient out by staying too long. Nobody teaches Hospital Visit 101.

I recently had this awkwardness brought home again. A dear friend on an island in Puget Sound had a stroke and was airlifted to a hospital in Seattle, where she had surgery to remove the clot. After Valerie was out of the ICU and discharged home for PT, I waited a few days before I phoned. Her husband, John, answered, sounding robust and cheerful, and immediately handed the phone to Valerie. I was reassured when she recognized my voice, but then the conversation dropped off abruptly because my dear friend couldn't find words, and the struggle bothered her. "How about this?" I asked finally. "You listen and I'll talk. It'll be easier." She seemed relieved. So, I deeply understand how difficult it can be for healthy people to interact with patients.

The morning of my next frightening surgery—abdominal this time—Karen, who'd brought that delicious pot roast for Ed after my first surgery, did the most amazing thing: she sent Marcelo Gindlin, the Argentinian cantor from her temple. Marcelo sat by my bedside, holding my hand, and then he started singing. His beautiful tenor voice, the one that usually soared up and filled an entire temple, now filled my dinky, drab room and drifted out to the hospital hallway, and the most amazing thing happened. As he began singing the second verse of "Byado" (*My soul I give to you*), I was bathed in a golden light. You could say I was hallucinating, but I wasn't, and I hadn't been given a pre-op sedative either.

Before Marcelo started singing, he suggested I bathe myself in golden light. I know this might sound as hokey as waving a magic wand, but in that moment, golden light was what I needed. Afterward, when I ran this by Jonathan, my internist, he said, "It makes sense. In that scary pre-op state, your brain was open to receiving information that could protect you."

Marcello was still singing, his operatic voice still filling the room when the technician arrived to transport me down to surgery. Ed accompanied me on one side, and as the technician pushed the gurney down the hallway, into the elevator, and out of the elevator, and then lined me up outside the OR, I was floating, still basking in the powerful feeling of being swathed in a halo of protective light. Instead of feeling scared and jittery, or undone by the institutional coldness of the hospital hallways, I was calm and at peace because of a most unusual musical narcotic delivered by an unexpected savior.

I told one of the doctors, "I am golden light."

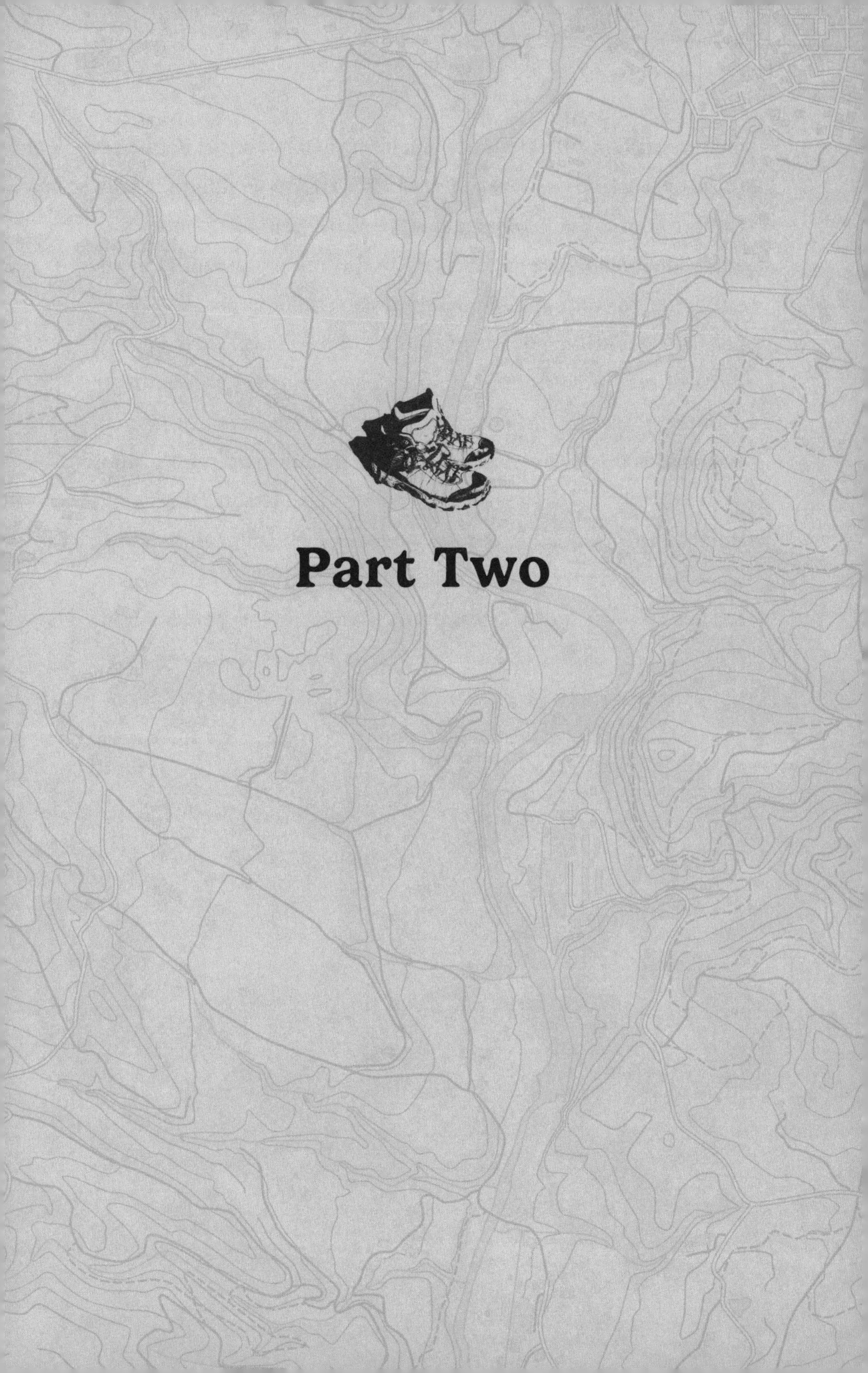

Part Two

CHAPTER 14

CEO of the Jo Recovery Team

The last and best thing Fred, the surgeon who botched my surgery, did was introduce me to C.O.R.E.—Center of Restorative Exercise.

Late on a Thursday afternoon in August, 274 days after The Accident and eighty-three days after the abdominal surgery, the 101 Freeway was slammed with rush-hour traffic. It looked like the iconic LA freeway photo where there are twenty lanes across, bumper to bumper. Such a hellish drive was not a promising beginning. The C.O.R.E. facility is in Northridge. Northridge! That's like asking someone from LA to drive to London. "I'll do it this once," I grumbled.

I wasn't driving myself. I wasn't strong enough. And my concern wasn't only about the horrendous traffic. I'd already been to three PT clinics, and those sessions had been a waste of time, energy, and hope. (Remember Carol saying, "You're going to be compromised for the rest of your life.") I didn't know what to expect that day, but what I would encounter was something most people will never experience their entire lives—paralyzed patients with spinal cord injuries, striving to walk again.

The driver pulled into the handicap-access parking space and dropped me off at what looked from the outside like a regular gym. I limped toward the front door and paused, taking a big breath to strengthen myself before shuffling in. It didn't look or sound like any regular gym population. Three people arrived in wheelchairs. I hobbled past a guy who was hanging by his waist in a huge overhead contraption that I'd learn is called a Biodex gait trainer. I'd also learn he hadn't walked for seventy-three days.

As I sat in the waiting area, a man passed by aggressively holding onto hiking sticks, but he wasn't hiking. I asked the woman next to me why she was there. She pointed to the teenage boy strapped upright into the EasyStand, a device used by people who have a neurological condition and can't stand on their own. "That's my son," she said.

"What happened?"

"Car accident."

A young woman on a nearby therapy table was maybe eighteen or nineteen, with long, glossy, brown hair and the most beautiful face. She was paralyzed, a quadriplegic. She'd been in a traffic accident and her boyfriend had died. I was tempted to distance myself. What am *I* doing here, with *these* people? But I wanted to walk again.

My appointment was with Taylor Isaacs, the founder of C.O.R.E., who showed me into a private evaluation room where the walls were a welcoming red tone, intentionally creating a warm, not medicinal, atmosphere. A life-size anatomical skeleton, Myra, stood nearby. Speaking in the delightful, clipped accent of a man born in Britain and raised in South Africa, Taylor asked me, "Do you feel normal?"

I sadly shook my head and dug around in my purse to find a business card for my new book: the attractive cover of the book was on the front, my author photo on the back. "That's me when I was healthy and normal," I said, pointing to the fresh image of a radiant person, brimming with life in her favorite red eyelet shirt and candy red lipstick. "I look in the mirror now and I look pale and sickly, not like myself. The person you're seeing today, this is not me."

If you are what you wear, then the dull and drab clothes I wore that late afternoon—old khaki shirt, baggy pants, certainly not my usual meet-and-greet costume—broadcasted my frazzled emotional and physical state.

I sat on a raised examination table, legs stretched directly in front of me, with Taylor on my right. "In thirty-three years of clinical practice, I've never worked with anyone without an Achilles," he said. "This is exciting. I can take all my education and put it into practice."

Taylor, who was getting an interdisciplinary doctorate degree in health promotion and human performance, had chosen the word "restore" carefully when he named his clinic—Center of *Restorative* Exercise. To him, it means physical *and* emotional restoration.

"Please, bend your foot up and back." When I could do that, he demonstrated on Myra, the skeleton, how the ankle is connected to the knee. "Let's not focus on that one Achilles. Lots of other muscles are responsible for plantar flexion, and yours are intact. The best analogy is flying a plane with four engines. If two engines blow, you can still fly and land the plane."

I let out an audible, full-body sigh of relief. This man, Taylor, was so refreshingly positive and encouraging.

He ran his hand down the front of my left foot and showed me that the other muscles that move the joint were intact. "Thank God, there's no nerve damage like in a spinal cord injury. That's when the brain sends a message to the muscle, to the nerves, but nothing happens. The very best news is that yours is one hundred percent orthopedic!"

"That's good news?" I asked, staring at him in disbelief. I'd been orthopedically challenged for 274 days, and so far, nothing about that experience had seemed like good news.

At that first consultation, I didn't know that most of the patients at C.O.R.E. suffered from spinal cord injuries *and* traumatic brain injuries with nerve involvement, which resulted in their not being able to walk.

Taylor explained that a biomechanist looks at the joint. "I'm very much a systemic anatomist," he said. "Nothing gets injured separately, and nothing heals separately. Everything in the body is completely interrelated and interdependent."

That was my *aha!* moment. I felt I could work with this person because we shared a similar philosophy. This whole-body interconnectedness struck home when the Achilles and the infection and the necrosis had set off a medical maelstrom beyond my ankle.

Taylor's knowledge was personal and hard-earned. This six-foot-three former professional soccer player for the Johannesburg Rangers had shattered his ankle during a match. He'd had three ankle surgeries, three back surgeries, six knee surgeries, and three hip/groin surgeries. He had once spent three months in the same hospital where I'd had my abdominal surgery, and he'd lost seventy-four pounds. In sharing his stories, he wasn't doing one-upmanship; he was sharing his traumatic personal medical history and his path to recovery. During the years it had taken him to fight his way back—he still wore a medical icepack over his sciatic region—he had discovered his mission: as a kinesiologist and strength and training specialist, he wanted to help severely injured people rebuild their bodies and regain their health, happiness, and life.

C.O.R.E. isn't a big, noisy gym like Gold's in Venice where Ed and I had worked out for years, a place known for its macho bodybuilders like Arnold Schwarzenegger. Instead, it's a smaller, more intimate, more personal facility, with just six professional therapists who work one-on-one with each client. It's unique in that C.O.R.E. bridges the gap between physical therapy and independent fitness.

On that first visit, I was desperate to walk normally again, and as I'd limped in, I'd glimpsed a few patients. One man had rolled in on a motorized wheelchair that he was belted into, another used one of those walking canes with prongs for stability, and another had three therapists working with him and was strapped into an Evolv EasyStand, a vertical device to hold him upright as he "walked." I only glanced at these individuals. It didn't seem polite to stare. With its soft, respectful murmur, this was a seriously sobering place. It wasn't your neighborhood gym where folks pop in to tone their abs or strengthen their biceps. There was no loud groaning and grunting, no high fives and back-slapping, no jazzy, pumping-iron music playing. Fred suggesting C.O.R.E. was his admission of how grave my situation was.

Although I was loath to admit it and would have liked to distance myself from this population, my being there was also an admission that whether I liked it or not, I was a member of this severely disabled population.

"You're an anomaly," said Taylor. "You're not a regular patient."

Taylor was an anomaly, too. He wore a black baseball cap with a tiny bun of hair tucked at the nape of his neck, and always a soccer shirt—today's was from C.D. Guadalajara, a Mexican soccer team. After an exhaustingly thorough two-hour evaluation, we exited the private room, and he asked me to please walk across the floor. A stepladder had been drawn on the floor with strips of red tape. Each rung represented an invitation to take and count another step.

"If I go too fast, my left calf cramps up and I'll shriek in pain, and I'll have to stop and shake it out."

On my gait analysis, Taylor, a data-driven professional, recorded that I'd done fourteen steps, six meters in 10.3 seconds.

Back in the quiet of the evaluation room, he proposed a plan: joint stabilization, isolated strength training and cardio-respiratory conditioning, total-body integrated strength training, and soft-tissue medical massage of myofascial connective tissue.

"We take a 360-degree approach at C.O.R.E. We don't leave a stone unturned. This is your blueprint," he said.

"How long will this take?" I asked, rubbing the spasm out of my left calf.

"How far do you want to go?" he asked.

"I want to be back to normal."

"You should think of yourself as CEO, chief energy officer of the Jo Recovery program," he said. "At this stage, you can come to

C.O.R.E. twice a week. When you get stronger, three times."

Regarding people confronting hardship, Frank Bruni writes, "There's a crucial period, a discrete phase, when they summon the will to steer toward a sunny horizon or they don't."*

That was my moment. I was on a new path. Again. Recovery was my full-time job, and Taylor was my head coach.

---

* Frank Bruni, *Born Round: A Story of Family, Food, and a Ferocious Appetite* (Washington, DC: National Geographic Books, 2010).

CHAPTER 15

The World's Largest Waterfall

One hundred and five days before The Accident.

The Ugly American is a pejorative term that depicts citizens exhibiting loud, arrogant, self-absorbed behavior. At the world's largest waterfall, I discovered the Ugly South American.

During a visit to South America, I was disgusted when I found myself among that ugly group of pushing, shoving, rude tourists whose only interest was in photographing themselves in front of the largest waterfall in the world.

A waterfall junkie must experience the largest waterfall in the world. Right? Not Niagara Falls but Iguazu Falls. This stupendous waterfall on the northern border between Argentina and Brazil stretches 1.7 miles—8,858 feet—across the top compared with Niagara's mere 3,947 feet. Who has ever thought of Niagara as dinky, right? Iguazu dwarfs Niagara in height as well: 269 feet versus Niagara's 167. After Eleanor Roosevelt saw Iguazu Falls, she said, "My poor Niagara . . ."

When Ed and I got together, we were on a new path too, which included six grandchildren. I had always thought if I had kids, I'd be their playmate. I'd take them on adventures. Instead, seven years of infertility (and a bad first marriage) had robbed me of having my own children, but being a grandmother to Ed's six grandchildren offered a huge bonus. Early on, we established a tradition of taking the grandkids on individual adventures. By the time it was our youngest grandson's turn, we seized on the idea of visiting Iguazu, and since Myles and I speak Spanish, we thought it could be educational. From early on, Myles was exceptional. Once, when he was still in diapers, he'd climbed up the rungs of our wooden banister, and on his way up to the second floor, dangling from the stair rungs about six feet up, he looked down at where I was reading in the living room, and said, "No responsible adult would let me do this." Yes, Myles actually said that while still in diapers. During that same visit, he played Checkers with Ed and was introduced to Ed's favorite chess set. Barely a few years later, the three of us were at a crosswalk, and as Ed pressed the button so the light would change, little Myles, always precocious, said, "You know that's a placebo."

We flew to Sao Paulo, Brazil, and then to Iguazu with Myles, who was twelve at the time. We had pages and pages of seriously notarized anti-kidnapping papers signed by both his parents indicating that we, the grandparents, had permission to take Myles Cardwell Warren out of the country. (In the summer of 2018, kidnapping for ransom was at its peak in Argentina.)

After we checked into the hotel, since our rooms weren't ready, we hung out by the pool. In the glaring sunlight, lounging by that huge, glistening, turquoise pool with dozens of loud guests nearby,

I gazed up at the three-story, pastel pink stucco building. "If we didn't know we were in the Brazilian jungle," I said to Ed, "we could mistake this for a garish hotel in Las Vegas."

Since ours was the only hotel in Iguazu National Park and the trailhead to the falls was barely a three-minute walk from the hotel's entrance, guests could explore the falls before the public started arriving at nine o'clock. The next morning, I was so gung-ho that I went into the adjoining room and awakened Myles. In the early morning fog, the three of us ran across the hotel's grassy front yard—this was three months before The Accident, and I could still sprint. We raced across the street that had no traffic and started down the boardwalk. With thirty thousand gallons of water crashing every second, the falls were lit in a dreamy, soft light with puffy white clouds billowing overhead. Except for a small maintenance crew and a handful of other early-bird hotel guests, we had the biggest waterfall in the world all to ourselves. I snapped a photo of Myles in front of the falls with a sunrise rainbow cresting over his head.

The parkland surrounding the falls is home to several animals: the *coatimundi*, a cute racoon-like animal, is also called the ring-tailed coati because of the rings on his long, fat tail; the toucan, with its distinctive and striking yellow-orange beak is so ubiquitous that we stopped paying special attention to this colorful bird that's unique to the rainforests of northern Argentina. Ed disliked the ugly vultures that swooped overhead, floating on the thermals from the falls.

We returned for the hotel's get-fat buffet breakfast, and then headed back to the falls. The jungle had awakened, and even though it was their winter, it was hot and humid, and the toucans were croaking. Since you can't drive your own car into the park unless you're staying at the hotel, at nine o'clock sharp, a parade of yellow school busses started disgorging tourists. Unfortunately, they would continue pouring out a crush of tourists all day. The boardwalk we had enjoyed mostly by ourselves was now packed solid, shoulder to shoulder. I grabbed onto Myles, who was barely five feet tall, and never let go of his blue sweatshirt. We were able to locate Ed because he was head and shoulders above the throng.

I wanted to return to the splashdown, called Devil's Throat, where we'd been earlier. But now the boardwalk was so packed, five and six deep, everyone jostling with their cell phones held high to capture a panoramic selfie of themselves in front of the falls. You could barely hear the roar of water falling for the clicking of all the shutters. Had Iguazu gotten Facebooked, or had it always been like this? There was such a traffic jam of people that we could not move. It was disgusting and numbing. And none of these loud, self-important tourists seemed interested in being quiet enough to stop and savor the extraordinary magic of the present moment—the stupendous roar of water falling. They were too busy elbowing each other out of the way so they could get to the front and smile for their picture. We couldn't wait to get out of there.

"Instead of being called Iguazu, it should be called, it's-a-zoo!" said Myles.

We weren't being hoity-toity about tourists. We were tourists too, but there were only three of us. An overwhelming sight over-crowded with tourists is underwhelming.

At Iguazu, we had the freedom to up and leave, to get ourselves out of that messy throng and do something else—play chess, play

Scrabble, take a tango lesson. We could just walk out and not return. A year later at C.O.R.E., I had no such choice. I'd just arrived, and to get "better," to walk again, I needed to hunker down and stay for the long haul.

Professionally, when I come up with a new idea for a book, a radio story, or a documentary, the spark gets me excited. *This'll be fun!* I think, and I throw myself into the work with enthusiasm. That wasn't how I felt about this new "project" at C.O.R.E. I was glad I had a plan—a comprehensive one—and a coach, but I'd already been at this Achilles business for nine months. My approach was more matter-of-fact: Okay, this is interesting. I'll go here, then I'll go there, and we'll see. I never considered not following Taylor's blueprint, and once I signed on, it would have been out of character not to give it my all.

Over the next few weeks, Taylor changed the blueprint and, in a hard-core press, insisted I add more modalities to the Jo Recovery Team: podiatrist, medical acupuncturist, an EMG/Nerve Conduction Study to identify damage to the nerves, and a myofascial release specialist to break up scar tissue. There wasn't a support group for this malady—AA doesn't stand for Achilles Anonymous—so to hold off the creeping depression of still being orthopedically challenged, I added a psychologist I'd seen before.

I understand this might sound like an expensive rehab program more suited for a professional basketball player like Kevin Durant—a pricey prescription for what Durant had to do for a year to get back on the court after his Achilles injury. And remember, Durant still had an Achilles. Taylor said it broke his heart that for some patients their insurance only covered a few sessions and then they had to stop and leave C.O.R.E. On this otherwise unlucky journey, I was lucky I had good insurance and a backup ability to take care of those modalities not covered. As a self-employed writer, I was also in charge of my own schedule. (I'd learned from my father, a self-employed inventor, that BOSS is a four-letter word.) And since Ed was retired, he was available in ways he wouldn't have been when he was still practicing law at the demanding level he'd worked in DC. I'd been the cook in the family, so where had all our meals come from during this time? I don't remember. I do remember a particularly pleasurable incident of having awkward but wonderful sex with my left leg elevated.

My days were filled with appointments, and they became my workload—with an emphasis on "load," as in heavy load. Every day, I was driven to see another professional on my Recovery Team. Howard Liebeskind, who was also the podiatrist for the Lakers, always started our session in a self-aggrandizing way, telling me what he'd just done for the team. I would listen, impatiently. What did I care about the Lakers? Ditch the Lakers. I wanted him to focus on me and my situation. What could he could do for *me*?

When I twirled my foot in circles, he said, "See, you're not supposed to be able to do that! You puzzle and dazzle me. You're my miracle patient."

I bent my foot up. "Dorsiflexion," I said.

"You have Achilles response," he said.

"I have no Achilles. I can show you the color picture of it being dead and curled up," I said. "Taylor says it's the other eight tendons in the front of my foot kicking in."

"The extensor tendons. You've got dorsiflexion," Howard said, flexing my foot. "It's compensatory action." Bending my foot down, he added, "Plantar flexion. You've got pretty significant function."

"I don't understand."

"Young lady, you had a disaster, and you're kicking butt!"

This professional might have been dazzled by how well I was doing, but I was not. I did not feel like I was kicking butt. I still felt marginalized and nowhere near where I wanted to be. I still had to be driven to most of these appointments because I didn't have the strength to drive there, find a parking space, park the car, exit the car, limp into the medical building, find the elevator, proceed down the hallway, finally locate the doctor's office, wait for the doctor to see me, endure the appointment, and then repeat all these steps in reverse to get back home. You might think, *What's the big deal? A few doors, some hallways.* But I didn't have the strength to drive and do all that, too.

"Look," I said to the podiatrist, "my flaccid left calf has atrophied so much that it flaps around like loose skin." The muscular Misty Copeland calves I'd developed from childhood years of ballet and ice-skating had vanished on my left side. In contrast, my right side still had a ballerina leg with an athletic calf.

Howard pulled out a standard-issue black cotton brace. While he laced it up, he said, "I've been a podiatrist for forty years, and I've never seen a situation like yours."

"Nobody has," I said. "That's why I'm going to see Kennedy in New York."

"Why are you seeing Kennedy?" His tone was pejorative, as in *Kennedy's a surgeon and you're not going to have surgery.*

"I'm gathering information on my options," I said. "Maybe I'm a candidate for an Achilles tendon transplant." Wearing the new brace, I started down his hallway. "It really helps!" I grinned as I headed back toward him. "What else do you have to offer?"

Howard had already started cutting a roll of black kinesiology tape to fit around my ankle and run up my calf. The ugly black tape looked forbiddingly sinister, but he said it might provide some stability.

Dr. Steve Chee, who was an acupuncturist and a medical doctor, wasn't sure what he could offer. His office was in a medical building, and his place was super clean, just like you'd want an operating room to be. There was a small sink in the corner where he washed his hands in front of me.

Holding my left foot, he said, "You're developing neuropathy in your heel."

"My mom used a walker because of neuropathy. Maybe if she'd had acupuncture…"

"How old was she when she developed it?"

"About ninety-five."

"If you're ninety-five and come in here with neuropathy…" he laughed.

He thought he could release the nerve entrapment on my heel, and maybe reduce the numb, thick, leathery patch that had formed there. He said I should try pumice on it. Pumice? Something as simple as drugstore pumice might help? A few months earlier, I couldn't stand to look at that yucky area down there or touch it. Now

I'm supposed to pumice my heel. I guess I could do that.

Wearing a hospital gown, I lay face down on Dr. Chee's table. He touched different parts of my ankle with his hand and asked if I could feel it. Here? There? Here? On my leathery left heel, I felt nothing. He inserted the acupuncture needles, one by one, and when he got closest to where the Achilles had been, I shrieked so loud—*SHIT!*—you could've heard me from where you're reading this.

After Dr. Chee got all the needles in, he very slowly turned on the electricity, one needle at a time. "Can you feel this?" he asked. His manner was patient, kind, thoughtful. He didn't rush.

"Nope."

"Now?"

"Nope." And then I screamed bloody murder.

"Breathe in and out."

As I lay there, face down, with all the needles inserted and electrified, I turned on a podcast as a distraction: *This American Life*, where I'd done some work. I asked him to leave the door open because I'm too claustrophobic to be in such a small room with the door shut, with needles in me. He left a bell for me to ring just in case. By the time Dr. Chee returned, I'd fallen asleep—or passed out.

At the next session with Taylor, as I worked alternate legs on the leg press machine, I complained that the acupuncturist was all the way in Beverly Hills. "That's a huge drive. Do you know how long it takes me to get there?"

"This is your job now," he said. "If you can't fly, then run. If you can't run, then walk. If you can't walk, then crawl. But whatever you do, you keep moving forward. That's Martin Luther King Junior."

He asked me to walk across the room as he videotaped me. "Please, take a proper good walk like you're going to meet a friend."

Unlike at Iguazu Falls, here at C.O.R.E., I wasn't a spectator taking photos; now I was the person being recorded. I was the center of attention, and even before I took the first step on the "ladder" taped on the floor, it didn't feel good. I pictured Lana on the far side of the room, and I was happy about meeting a favorite friend, but I wasn't happy being videotaped. Even before I stepped off on my good foot, I felt I would fail at this task, and Taylor would have a lasting record of my failure.

Barefoot, I set off nervously, feeling the pressure to perform. Now the task of walking normally across a regular room felt like a walk too far. I "walked" but it was more like lurching and limping. "The walking's not good," I called back from the other side of the room, my voice rife with disappointment and defeat. I shook my head, sad and upset about still being hobbled. "I'm just not walking right." I didn't ask to see the video. I didn't need to. I knew I looked wobbly, unsteady, unsure, pounding my right foot down to steady my left foot.

A man, middle-aged, had been sitting nearby, strapped into a custom motorized wheelchair, which he would never get out of. He said, "Looks good to me."

I nodded at him, acknowledging his observation, which stopped me cold because everything's relative, isn't it? I couldn't walk like I used to, but I also wasn't belted into a wheelchair for life.

Some friends visited recently for Sunday lunch at the beach. One of them, Joel, had Stage 4 prostate cancer; it had metastasized to his lungs and lymphatic system. Although he was being seen at the City of Hope, his outlook was not hopeful. He barely lived another year, and we were invited to his memorial service. In stark contrast, my recovery was super difficult, but I wasn't dying, Ed didn't need to prepare a funeral, and I wasn't paralyzed for life.

CHAPTER 16

How's the Skiing?

"Physical therapists are very noble people, but they're practicing in a broken system," Taylor said at our next session. "You go to PT, and then you're discharged, and where do you go? You go home, and you degenerate. I designed C.O.R.E. so you have continuity of care. Our formula for success: PET. Passion—does the client have the passion to recover? Energy—do they have the energy to put into recovery? And Time—do they have the time to put into recovery?"

I had PET nailed. Even though the drive was still a miserable, frightening eighty miles, two hours round trip on the race track of the Ventura Freeway—and now I was driving myself—I usually managed to show up early and have a good attitude. I wasn't a quitter.

Along with everything I was doing at C.O.R.E., Taylor also knew I had a doctor's appointment lined up in New York City. About this time, Kevin Durant, a player (then) with the Golden State Warriors, ruptured his Achilles in Game 5 of the 2019 NBA finals. This is considered one of the most debilitating injuries in basketball. (More than 75 percent of Achilles tendon ruptures occur during sports-related activity.)* I emailed my rambling medical history to Dr. Douglas L. Cerynik, the doctor mentioned in an article about Durant in *The Wall Street Journal*. Dr. Cerynik, who had coauthored a study about NBA players and Achilles injuries, had examined eighteen players who had suffered Achilles tendon ruptures, and his conclusion was bleak: It's rare for players who suffered from these injuries to return to their pre-injury form. Kevin Durant's remarkable recovery was an exception, but Durant still had an Achilles and I did not. I was no NBA player, but maybe I could be an exception, too.

Through Dr. Cerynik, I arranged an appointment with Dr. John G. Kennedy at the Foot and Ankle Center at New York University Langone Health. Taylor, who knew about my upcoming visit to New York, asked, "What do you hope to gain by this appointment?"

"I want to see if I'm a candidate for an Achilles tendon transplant."

On a brisk autumn morning 263 days after The Accident, Ed and I were in New York City. After brushing my teeth and getting dressed, all I wanted was to be teleported from our hotel in Soho to Kennedy's office a mile away at NYU Langone. This consultation was the entire, important, big point of my being wheelchaired through LAX, and our flying 2,475 miles to JFK. Randy Sherman, the trauma

---

* Dr. Douglas L. Cerynik, "The Big Gamble on Kevin Durant's Achilles Tendon," *Wall Street Journal*, July 3, 2019.

wound plastic surgeon, had once loomed as my next best hope. Now John G. Kennedy felt like my last best hope for a more ambulatory future.

Dr. Kennedy specializes in Achilles tendon transplants, so as we grabbed a quick breakfast in the hotel lobby, I said to Ed, "The good news is that maybe this doctor can get me a tendon from a cadaver—a deceased person, a dead cow, a frog."

"Calm down," said Ed, finishing his coffee. "Let's meet the guy and see what he has to say."

We had some time before my important appointment. While Ed was at the gym, I was too anxious to just sit there drinking more coffee, counting the minutes. Since walking has always cleared my head, I optimistically laced up the new brace the podiatrist had just given me, grabbed my hiking poles (yes, I brought my poles to New York City), and set off—tentatively. Mercer Street has the reputation of being a great walking street but quite uneven. No kidding. In this Soho neighborhood, the challenging cobblestone streets sent me wobbling. Thank God for the hiking poles. In Brazil, I'd been in a real jungle. Here, I was trekking in a concrete jungle where a lively parade of street vendors hawked jewelry, sunglasses, and hot dogs. I'd only gone a block, "hiking" Mercer Street, crossing Prince, gripping my poles for balance, when a man yelled across the four lanes of traffic on Broadway, "How's the skiing?"

I gave him a thumbs up. I didn't mind being mistaken for a street athlete trekking the wilderness of Manhattan instead of someone hobbled by a disability.

My phone pinged. It was Fred. Again. He'd been texting "How are you?" every few days, and it struck like a poison dart. Why didn't the guy leave me alone? As if his text was contagious, I instantly deleted it.

Dr. Kennedy, a tall, handsome Irishman, wore a crisp white shirt, red tie, and glasses shoved back on the top of his head. Before we sat down, he said, "Let's go out in the hallway and let me watch you walk."

In the public hallway, in my stockinged feet, I did my limping-lurching-loping routine. Again.

Back in an examination room, Dr. Kennedy held my injured foot in both of his hands, feeling the pulse almost as if the foot itself could communicate. This reminded me of my late husband, an internist, who practiced by the credo: Listen to the patient, and they'll tell you what's wrong; listen hard enough, and they'll tell you how to treat it. He was holding my foot as if he needed to touch it to make a decision.

Dr. Kennedy is a pioneer in microscopic Achilles tendon transplant surgery, and his easy-going, quick-to-smile manner was welcome in my serious situation. "I don't use cadaver donors," he said, "which can have a rejection factor."

"Right," I said. I'd wondered about that.

He showed us how he'd take one of three tendons from the big toe on my left foot and make it into an Achilles. Designer orthopedics.

He glanced at the black fabric brace I'd tossed on the chair next to Ed. "Get rid of it. Stop relying on that."

"I like it." I was a little offended because it felt like the brace was helping to keep me upright.

"Can she get along with no Achilles?" asked Ed, posing the central question of this consultation.

Dr. Kennedy said he had several patients with some pathology in their Achilles that kept them from having their tendon repaired. "Often these patients had a previous rupture whose repair failed." I nodded, identifying with that sorry predicament. "Or they had grafts that failed or became infected, and the risk of surgery outweighed the benefit. In all of those cases, the patients got back to walking, playing tennis . . ."

"Really?" I wanted to give him a hug. For the first time on this journey I was with a physician who had experience with patients who had no Achilles, and he said they were doing okay. I felt I was in the right place with the right professional.

The Achilles is surrounded by a tendon sheath, the paratenon. This is a diaphanous layer in the normal tendon. The paratenon has a blood supply and provides many of the growth factors for tendon repair and regeneration.

"In your case," said Kennedy, "your paratenon would have laid down scar tissue and some tendon-like material joining the remnants of your tendon. This will never have the same mechanical properties as a normal tendon, and most importantly, it can never function as a true Achilles, as the tendon scar unit will never have the same tension as a normal tendon, but it does allow up-and-down motion of your ankle."

"So, that's why I could dazzle the podiatrist with my plantar flexion." It felt like I'd been holding my breath since this consultation began, and now I began breathing again.

"This allows function but not normal function," he said, cautioning my enthusiasm.

The prevailing wisdom had been that all injured Achilles tendons required surgical repair. We learned that some countries—Japan and Canada—don't do Achilles reattachment surgery in most situations. "Work in Canada has shown that treatment without surgery can lead to the same long-term functional outcome with less complications," said Dr. Kennedy. "This is different from having no tendon, as in your case, but the biology is similar. The Achilles is an extraordinary tendon," he said, with admiration. "For too long, doctors have treated it in the same fashion, often with disappointing outcomes. Early weight-bearing, nonoperative booting, and the use of biologic adjuncts to stimulate tendon regeneration and repair are the way of the future, and surgical repair will be rare."

Surgeons like to do surgery, but after my ghastly necrosis and studying the mottled skin flap covering the sunken graveyard down there, this surgeon was not eager to do mine, and I was in no rush, either. Although Kennedy had loomed as my last, big, best important hope, it's curious that I wasn't unhappy or disappointed with this outcome. That's because post-op in New York City, I'd have to live there in a hotel, and I'd be back to square one: on the knee scooter, unable to walk again for another three months.

Wrapping up our session, Kennedy sat back. "Let's see how much function you can regain without surgery. For the next two months, keep a journal. Record the number of steps and how you felt taking them, continue PT, aggressive PT, and add shockwave therapy."

Shockwave therapy was developed for the ankles of horses. It was so successful in treating the painful ankles of racehorses that it's banned before races. After its success in the equine world, it moved into soft-tissue application in humans.

Before we left the office, a surgical fellow studying with Kennedy administered my first session of shockwave therapy. I changed into a hospital gown, and using a pneumatically driven device that made a loud *rat-a-tat* sound and looked like a clumsy hammer, the fellow started pounding around my wound. For ten minutes, I lay on my stomach, leg bent, and the treatment, which was mildly painful, delivered an acoustic wave that carried high energy to my ankle.

In the changing room, as I stripped off the hospital gown and dressed in my street clothes, I wondered if the session had helped. I had no idea. This device was used to treat pain in the ankles of horses, but I didn't have pain. (And I'm not a racehorse.)

Before leaving Kennedy's office, I checked to see if Susanne, his scheduler who had arranged my appointment, had arrived. A beautiful, fortyish blond woman was at the desk where I'd left the flowers. We hugged and kissed like old friends.

"You didn't have to bring flowers," she said.

"That's the least I could do. He's the first and only doctor I've met who has helped patients in my condition. He said I should check back in two months."

It was much more fun checking in with our grandchildren. On another adventure, this one in Iceland with Finn, thirteen, we had a kicky experience at Seljalandsfoss. Although Iceland has hundreds of waterfalls, this is one of the few in the world that has a footpath *behind* the falls. Wearing cheap clear-plastic raincoats we'd just purchased in the parking lot (think Saran Wrap), the three of us started on the 1.2-mile loop. Because of the slick wet stones, we stepped very carefully behind the falls. Standing in that hollow, cave-like space, we looked straight out. Directly in front of us, just inches away, sixty feet of freezing cold water was falling forcefully, close enough to get us sopping wet in spite of our flimsy raincoats. It was totally exhilarating, and I felt so pumped up, alive, and wet!

Our Icelandic adventure was 107 days before The Accident. I was still sure-footed, and the scariest thing for me was watching Ed. Because of his artificial right ankle and lifelong issues with balance, he made it through that dangerously slippery, muddy, rocky downhill trail behind the falls only because at a crucial moment when he slipped, he grabbed onto the back of our thirteen-year-old grandson's coat and piggybacked on his shoulders. In *Will to Wild*, Shelby Stanger describes a "trail angel" as someone who arrives just when you need them most to offer a helping hand. Finn was Ed's trail angel.

We also sampled local Icelandic specialties: Finn and Big E tasted (and spit out) fermented shark, which was so stinky you could smell it a block away; I ordered a sheep's head, the whole head. I wondered if that grossed Finn out, watching me knife and fork into the roasted head of a sheep.

There was no fermented shark, no sheep's head for breakfast the morning after my appointment with Dr. Kennedy. Instead, Ed and I had a lovely, long, leisurely breakfast at Balthazar. With its red leather banquettes and towering flower arrangements, it reminded me of the old Russian Tea Room on West 57th Street. Now that I'd had my all-important doctor's appointment, I could breathe again, so we treated ourselves to a few days in the city. I was comfortable in New York. In my twenties, I'd lived on the Upper West Side and worked at WNBC-TV at Rockefeller Center and WNET at Columbus Circle, so I was happy having the chance to poke around in my old haunts. Who knows? Being my mother's daughter, maybe I'd get a new outfit to celebrate.

Sitting side by side at a small corner table, close enough that our thighs were touching, I turned to Ed. "I have something to tell you." I smiled. "Have I told you, this morning, how I feel about you?"

Eddie smiled, too. He knew what was coming. "You love me. I'm your favorite."

"I want to live the rest of my life with you and die in each other's arms one night."

I kissed him. How could a person navigate a serious medical journey like this alone?

Recently, I'd had lunch with a friend who was going through some medical problems, alone, all by herself. Shelby's new cardiologist had diagnosed a weak heart (whatever that means) and said she'd be on meds for the rest of her life. She also needed cataract surgery in both eyes. I commiserated with her and told her how hard it is to go through medical situations by yourself. She agreed and said she'd been listless and tired, and was nodding off in the afternoons. She also quickly added that she was really okay, that growing up as an only child, she had grown accustomed to self-soothing. As Shelby finished her chopped salad with extra ranch dressing, she held back tears, and I poked at my mediocre fish and chips. I don't think she convinced either of us that going through two cataract surgeries alone was gonna be a breeze.

Friends comfort each other in different ways. After my previous husband died, when I was still keening in grief, Annie paid a visit. We sat in my living room, across from each other, and Annie held my feet. Sometimes no words will work; only a soothing touch from a friend helps.

Back in our New York hotel room, I dug ice cubes out of a wine bucket and dropped them into a Ziplock bag. Sitting on the couch with my leg elevated on the coffee table and ice cubes on my ankle, I didn't feel like I'd regressed to square one—elevating and icing—because I'd also been given new tasks: continue aggressive PT, add shockwave therapy, and keep track of my steps and how I feel taking them.

My journal entries would be all over the place:

> *7,836 steps, about 3.4 miles, I feel very happy, happier than I've been in a long time. Feeling positive.*

> *559 steps—had to stop walking after ten minutes, no strength, every day is different... disappointed but not discouraged.*

From our hotel, I spotted a mass of colorful umbrellas that I hoped was an arts and crafts fair, exactly what I like. It turned out to be a food fair, and it hadn't opened yet. By 11:10 a.m., after resting on the front stoops of several brownstones, I barely made it back to our hotel—2.2 miles, 5,037 steps. It reminded me of four months earlier in Austin at the Pecan Street Festival. *I cannot walk!* This time, I was disappointed about the present but positive about the future. Why? How could I feel optimistic when I'd just collapsed again? Because Kennedy had told us about patients in a situation similar to mine who had gotten back to walking, playing tennis. Maybe this wasn't going to be my condition forever. Maybe I wasn't going to be an *ex*-hiker.

On the way back from scoping out the fair, wearing my dependable HOKAs I passed a store selling gorgeous, feminine shoes—black heels with a sassy bow on the front. I couldn't wear them now, but maybe I could soon.

On our way home, I trekked with my hiking poles through Newark Airport: 3,976 steps, and I felt okay.

CHAPTER 17

The Teddy Bears' Picnic

My life hadn't always been about counting steps and meeting new doctors. Often life had been playful and silly, like in Montana after we had the bear in the house and I couldn't resist the life-size, stuffed bears that were on sale at Costco. On a visit one summer, the grandkids—Myles, seven, and Finn, nine—immediately attached themselves to the bears. Myles was the smarty-pants in the family, who solved advanced mathematical puzzles in his head for fun with Ed. I always thought Finn would be some kind of therapist when he grew up because he was already, even at nine, so naturally attuned to other people's feelings.

One morning, Myles was at the kitchen counter eating crepes with powdered sugar sprinkled on top, the kind my grandmother had made for me and now I was making for our grandkids. The blond bear, who Myles had named Blondie, was seated next to him, wearing a red cowboy hat. Finn was snuggling with the brown bear, Brownie, and Chloe, eleven, was pretending to have outgrown these little-kid shenanigans.

After gulping down breakfast, and with flecks of powdered sugar still on his chin, Myles turned to Finn, "Let's have another race!"

Myles threw Blondie across one of the ottomans and dove on top—he'd be riding "bearback." The ottomans had well-oiled rollers, and he pumped hard with both feet as he sped *fast* across our slick wooden floors. Finn jumped on the other ottoman. The competition was on.

Bumper car–style—*whoosh! bam! bang!*—Finn bombed alongside Myles, almost slamming both of them into the coffee table. The competitors *crashed* to a stop as they *slammed* into the couch in front of the window in the living room. Yes, the wooden floors were getting banged up, but that was a small price to pay for the kids having so much fun. The boys stepped on it again—this time *flying* into the kitchen and *skidding* into the center island.

Finn invented a more dangerous trick. He carefully, like an engineer, positioned his ottoman in line with the swing in our living room. (Yes, we have a swing in our living room. Maybe it's an homage to the swings I'd loved in Seward Park as a child.) Standing on the swing, he pumped and pumped until he was way high up in the air, and then daredevil-style, he boldly made a flying leap, diving directly onto the ottoman, which instantly rocketed him and the ottoman clear across the room. In that mini-second when he was suspended in midair before making a safe landing, if Finn felt scared, he didn't show it.

While the boys were still flying around on the ottomans—they could've done this all day—Ed and I decided that all of us needed another activity. I suggested a picnic. Picnic is one of my favorite words. I like the way it sounds—PIK+nik—and what it represents: enjoying food outdoors with friends.

"Can we bring the bears?" asked Myles, looking up from his ottoman.

"Yes!" said Finn. "Please!"

At least they didn't want to bring the ottomans. "If you carry them, you can bring them," said Ed.

"Okay, we're going to Fairy Lake!" I said. "There are fairies there."

"Ferries?" said Chloe. "A ferry boat goes across the lake?"

"No, *fairies*," I said. "Like with wings, fairies that fly."

"Real fairies?" said Myles and Finn in unison, wide-eyed.

"You'll see."

Five years later, life was no picnic. The best possibility of my being able to return to Montana and Fairy Lake rested in strictly following the rigorous blueprint from C.O.R.E. where the helpful fairies were of a different sort. After parking in the handicapped spot, I limped in and waved at Danea at the front desk and said good morning to Brittney, the office manager.

"How are you feeling today?" asked Taylor, his standard opening line.

"Okay," I said. "I want to get better," which was also my standard opener.

I was doing the BAPS board at home. The BAPS—Biomechanical Ankle Platform System—is a thick, flat, blue plastic disc that rests on the floor and has five different axis points. The idea is to engage your ankle by moving your foot side to side, front to back, and in circles.

"I'd like to do it standing but it's too challenging. I have to do it sitting down, which is disappointing. It's sort of fun to do with my good leg, but with my bad leg…"

"We don't use those terms," interrupted Taylor. "Good leg, bad leg. We say 'involved' leg. Exercise is medicine, and we're focusing on possibility-based medicine. Anything is possible."

Taylor watched me walk and said, "You have an antalgic gait, a pain avoidance gait. You're a master compensator because 85 percent of your weight-bearing is on your right side. That's not a gap! That's a huge gap! That's the difference between a size 2 shoe and size 22. That's a gross asymmetry."

"I know *that*," I said, irritated, and also scared. I knew I was favoring my right side, which was throwing my whole body off-kilter. I was also starting to have compensatory pain in my right leg from over-using it.

The real giveaway about how much farther I had to go in my recovery was the simple single-leg stance. "Lookie here," said Taylor, pointing to a wall. "Stand against the wall for safety, please." Good manners were another hallmark of Taylor's unique style.

On my right leg I could stand for two minutes easily. "Excellent!" said Taylor.

"I cannot stand on my left leg," I said, quickly grabbing onto a nearby chair.

Over many months my balance progressed, slowly, from stable to unstable, supported to unsupported. First, I'd do the simplest exercise lying on my stomach, a swimming-like movement that I wouldn't have considered "exercise" in my previous life. Then several weeks later, I progressed to doing the same baby swimming movement standing with my back against the wall, with the goal being to move away from the wall when I was stronger. I'd do these movements unloaded, with no weights, and then loaded, adding a one-pound hand weight, a dinky weight that was all I could manage because even adding a mere sixteen ounces threw me off-balance.

I was totally micro-focused on my own exercises, but I was also curious about the other patients, and would sneak shy glances at them. I was fascinated by Michael, who'd been an LAPD cop and had a stroke, and was relearning how to walk. Maybe Michael wouldn't like my saying this, but this man in his fifties now looked like a crippled toddler trying to take his first baby steps. He'd throw his left leg out to the side and then try to cobble a step together. It was embarrassing and painful to watch. Once, as he was muttering to himself, "Spastic, my arm's spastic today," he looked over at me and asked, "Nothing neurological?"

"Nope, all orthopedic."

When we were on the far side of the room, I whispered to Taylor, "How do other people feel about being here?"

"I'm in a profession where no one wants to be here. I know that," he said. "People are here by circumstance, not choice."

On our way to Fairy Lake, we piled into Ed's old blue Tahoe, the one with the dimpled exterior from the time I got caught in a bruising hailstorm. Chloe thoughtfully climbed into the wayback, and then Myles and Finn buckled up, and we handed them their bears, which they hugged as tightly as if they'd always been their besties.

Once when Ed and I were heading to LAX on our way to Montana, we had a driver from England. When he heard about the bear in our house and learned we were hosting a Fourth of July picnic for the neighbors, he said he had just the song for us. Then he burst into a wonderfully silly English children's song, "The Teddy Bears' Picnic":

If you go down in the woods today,
You're sure of a big surprise.
If you go down in the woods today,
You'd better go in disguise.
For every bear that ever there was
Will gather there for certain because
Today's the day the teddy bears have their picnic.

Fairy Lake is just up the road from our place, and the five of us kept singing and giggling as we headed up Bridger Canyon.

"Look," said Ed, "Sacagawea!"

The lake is located at the base of Sacagawea Peak, elevation 9,654 feet. Ed and I hiked up Sacagawea once, which is named for a Lemhi Shoshone Indian woman who accompanied the Lewis and Clark expedition. That was years ago, and hiking that stupendous mountain post-Accident would be a peak way too far.

As we bumped along the seven-mile dirt road to the lake, a brutal drive on a bad road, we continued belting out that happy song:

If you go down in the woods today . . .

"Why are these craters called potholes when they're deep enough to sink a tractor?" I grumbled to myself.

Warnings remind drivers to use four-wheel drive, that this dirt road is not suitable for an RV, and cars with low clearance will not fare well. No kidding. It's not open and is impassable in winter, but it was nearly impassable that summer day in August. I couldn't go slow enough or swerve fast enough to dodge all the sinkholes, but since Ed kept replaying the Teddy Bear song on his phone, we kept laughing as we bounced along and belted out:

> . . . Because *today's the day the teddy bears have their picnic!*

When the kids were younger, we had a car that gave out audible directions in a woman's voice. The kids had never been in a car with a navigational Destination Assist device, and I explained that it was Thelma. I said she was in the trunk, and when we arrived at our destination, I showed them Thelma, a doll in the trunk. On our way to Fairy Lake, Myles asked, "Is Thelma with us?"

The road to Fairy Lake was heavily forested with wildflowers in full bloom—lots of stately Queen Anne's lace and a low, blue groundcover that would have been bluebonnets if we'd been in Texas.

At last, the road dead-ended at the parking lot. I pulled into a space, punched off the ignition, and stopped gripping the steering wheel. We'd made it without bottoming out and getting stuck midair in one of those craters.

A wave of the loveliest evergreen forest aroma announced that we'd arrived at a totally different, wild place. Although Myles, the youngest, was wearing a big-boy T-shirt with DUDE on the front, he whined that he could not carry his bear. Big E carried his. As the seven of us entered the path into the forest—the five of us and the two stuffed bears—Myles ran ahead, hopping down the nearly vertical stairs to the lake, exactly how you'd expect a happy-go-lucky, frisky seven-year-old would skip ahead with no thought to safety and secure stepping. The rest of us, loaded with bears and blankets, took the gentler switchback.

The awe of Fairy Lake.

The first glimpse of Fairy Lake is powerful. Always. Its shimmering emerald green water—it could've been called Green Lake—with lodgepole pines growing up from the shoreline is a breathtaking wonder. Every time. How's it possible there's something this beautiful? Alice Waters, the famous chef at Chez Panisse in Berkeley, talks about experiencing something utterly beautiful for a brief moment and how we enter a state of awe. The magical beauty of Fairy Lake, where the water is so clear you can see to the bottom, instills in me a spiritual feeling of reverence.

Since this dazzling place was mostly empty, we easily found a spot to spread our blanket. Don't picture a flat public picnic area with tables and benches; we were on a slanted, semi-rocky slope with downed tree trunks. Myles sat on Blondie, sharing her with Big E as a back rest.

"Jo, are you okay?" Finn asked, which was Finn being Finn, always looking out for the other person. As he leaned against Brownie, he moved over to make room for me.

Chloe, who was in her craze where she only ate white food, was munching on popcorn. Since we had left in such a rush, the rest of us picnicked on Goldfish crackers and leftover chocolate muffins.

The boys skipped rocks, and Finn claimed his skipped fifty times. On the far side, a brave older boy was soaring way out over the lake on a rope swing. The easy 1.2-mile loop around the lake is much trickier than it looks because of the forested shoreline, fallen trees, and a slick, muddy bank. This adventure was five years before The Accident, and walking that tricky loop had been challenging but no problem.

As we relaxed, barely a few inches up from the freezing cold shoreline that sparkled in shimmering shades of emerald green, I told the kids about the fairies, how they dance in the air. "They rise directly up out of the water. They have gossamer wings. They dance like a flame."

"Real fairies?" The boys were intrigued. Squinting, they stared hard out into the water, trying to spot a fairy. Chloe gave me a skeptical look.

"Yes, like in *Peter Pan*. I've seen them here before." Don't we all need the magic of a fairy godmother, or godfather, stepping in and dropping a little fairy dust on us? "I don't see them every time we come, but most of the time." I explained that these tiny creatures with wings have magical qualities. "In Europe they live in enchanted forests." I looked around at the gorgeous green forest surrounding us. "This forest must be enchanted." I would have been totally happy coming up with more fairy stories. Think Tinker Bell, Sleeping Beauty. I was loving this make-believe playtime.

Fairy Lake is such a serene spot. Just hearing the water softly lapping at the shore, gazing out at the shimmering shades of green, and Sacagawea Peak towering overhead with snow still on its slopes, was a meditation.

I could have lingered longer, but how much serenity do kids want?

Connecting with serenity is a lot like finding those Lucky Stones I collect. The myth is that you cannot go in search of a Lucky Stone; you have to chance upon it by luck, serendipity. You can't go in aggressive search of serenity, either. But if you turn your phone off and happen to put yourself in the right spot—the waterfront at Fairy Lake where calm reigns—serenity can find you. It's said that wonder and awe can also improve your health, but my health was fine. Eventually, the powerful memory of Fairy Lake serenity would help in my recovery—it would provide an oasis of mental calmness in the troubled medical waters still ahead.

CHAPTER 18

You Look Normal

I was on treadmill at C.O.R.E., working up to 120 steps a minute, a regular walk-talk speed. Taylor was nearby with a laptop, recording my data. As usual, he was wearing one of his soccer shirts, this time from the FC Cincinnati team.

I could walk and talk without being short of breath, which was a good indicator of my progress. I said to Taylor, "Thanksgiving's coming, and I need to do a dress rehearsal with you." He looked confused. "So many people keep saying to me, 'You look normal. You're walking normal.' Or someone says, 'You look like you could run a marathon.' It makes me nuts. I want to say, 'What an idiot. Of course, I'm not walking normal! I'm limping and lurching! I only appear to be normal.'"

These remarks reminded me of what Lynda Wolters wrote in *Voices of Cancer*, in which she had a message for friends and family: "The phrase 'Now that you're back to normal . . .' is like a knife to the heart. We cannot compare our current state to where we were prior to our diagnosis. As patients, we must accept and recognize where we are now or we will go mad."*

I pressed STOP and, holding onto the handle, slowly and carefully stepped down from the Cybex treadmill. Facing Taylor, I said, "You say to me, 'You look normal,' and then we figure out my response. We're role-playing."

"Okay," he said. "How about this? Thank you for noticing. I'm working very hard learning to walk again. I'm glad you noticed my progress."

We both burst into smiles.

On my way out, I said good morning to Stephanie Mendoza, the new intern. She was working with a client who was struggling to walk, step by slow step, with a walker. Motioning to me, Stephanie said to her client, "She's a waterfall girl. She hikes to waterfalls."

A recent college grad when I'd met her a year ago, Stephanie was doing a visiting rotation at C.O.R.E. as part of her degree. Recently she'd been hired full-time, and she'd made the decision to devote her life to this population.

"How's it make you feel," I'd asked, "that most of these people will never walk again?" I was pretty sure how it would make me feel—sad.

"Everyone's goals are different," she'd said, with a maturity beyond her years. "Somebody may want to walk, and for somebody else, just being able to transfer from their car to the wheelchair may be their goal."

* Lynda Wolters, *Voices of Cancer* (Herndon, VA: Mascot Books, 2019).

At Thanksgiving with Ed's West Coast family, his son Zach carved the turkey by flashlight because the power had gone off. As Wendy, his wife, pulled the side dishes out of the oven by candlelight, I sat on the couch in front of the glowing fireplace next to our granddaughter, Chloe.

"You're doing really well," Chloe said to me.

Instead of snarling and thinking *she's an idiot*, I said, "Thank you. I'm working very hard on therapy, and thanks for noticing the improvement. I still have a long way to go."

Following Thanksgiving, I had my fifth and final shockwave therapy session. As I carefully removed my shoe and sock, Howard, as usual, was going on and on about the Lakers. His starting each session with the latest inside news about this basketball team for which he was the podiatrist always reminded me of someone with low self-esteem. As if the fame and importance of the Lakers would somehow rub off on this lowly podiatrist in West Hills.

As he started pummeling my heel, I lay back in the reclining chair, staring at the ceiling. This experience was uncomfortable enough without watching as this small guy with balding hair pounded at my heel. After about ten minutes, he switched off the awkward, loud device. I twirled my injured foot around in circles.

"See, you're not supposed to be able to do that!" he said. "I've never seen anyone in your condition do that."

"When I wake up, I do this." I twirled my involved foot in the opposite direction. "It used to hurt, like I was crunching through scar tissue. Now it hurts less."

As part of the Jo Recovery Team, I had a weekly appointment with Howard. Every time, he said I puzzled him. "Right now, I'm working extra hard with Taylor to see how much function I can regain," I said. Since Howard and Taylor worked with some of the same athletes, they knew each other. "If I regain enough function, maybe I don't have to return to New York and have another surgery."

I'd just passed the two-month mark, and I'd sent Dr. Kennedy an update and step count: 1,800 steps, and I'm riding the stationary bike; 3,996 steps 1.7 miles; 3,532 steps 1.2 miles. I said that since I was making some progress, maybe we could hold off on another visit.

Howard had custom orthotics made for me. We'd been waiting weeks and weeks to get them, and before he stuffed them in my shoes, he ran out of the room and came back with a huge pair that he'd made for one of the Lakers, as if a major athlete wearing orthotics would further convince me of their worth. He dug the standard insole out of my HOKAs and shoved in the stiff new orthotic.

"Try them out," he said. "Sometimes they don't get the arch right."

Leaning against the doorway, he watched and studied my gait as I started down the hall in his office.

I'm usually optimistic, but by this point on my journey, I wasn't expecting that anything would deliver much help. Let alone a ten-inch piece of stiff, black plastic shoved inside my shoe. But even after the very first step, I could tell something was different and much better. "Wow!" I smiled, standing tall, pushing my shoulders back. "My feet feel secure, like they're being held firmly in place. It's like my heel is locked in." The orthotics instantly felt right. A little piece of black plastic was making all the difference. I was still thumping my right foot down, but I didn't feel so wobbly, and I was beaming. "Wait until I tell Kennedy. Maybe with these I can do even more steps!" Feeling euphoric, I briskly passed Howard in his doorway, continued to the reception area, waved happily at his secretary, and turned back, eager to do it again. "This is far and away the best! Who knew something like this could make such a difference? Maybe I should've gotten these a long time ago?"

This business of recovery is a mysterious, never-ending dance.

CHAPTER 19

Don't Strive for Perfection but for Connection

In my wildest dreams, I never would have imagined that 380 days after The Accident, I'd be attending a Christmas party for people with disabilities. A notice on the front desk at C.O.R.E. announced a holiday party. I whispered to Taylor, "Will everyone be coming in their wheelchairs?"

"Yes."

Of course. What a stupid question.

The night of the party, Ed was in bed with a cold. I brought him up a Four Roses bourbon and tonic and a hamburger (no bun) and kissed him goodbye. Reluctantly, I left him alone as I went by myself to the party. Since the invitation said to bring a dish, I brought a fresh fruit salad. Colorful, healthy.

The 101 Freeway was even crazier with holiday traffic. As an eighteen-wheeler sped by at 80 mph in the fast lane, it made me so sick I pulled as far away as possible—because when that speedster driving a fifty-seven-foot rig like a race car crashed, any vehicle near him would be slammed. Since so many of the spinal cord patients at C.O.R.E. had been injured in traffic accidents, "traffic accident" had taken on a scarier meaning.

The parking lot at C.O.R.E., where I usually snagged a handicapped spot in front, was packed. I circled once, twice, and grew concerned I might have to head home until I finally scored a spot way in the back near the dumpsters.

I limped slowly across the dark parking lot and lingered outside, staring through the windows at the lively festivities going on inside and enjoying the Christmas music floating through the air. I felt like a spy. I'd never been to a party like this, and I hadn't known what to expect, especially since it was co-sponsored by the Triumph Foundation, which helps people triumph over paralysis. I wore a red velvet shirt with a cheerful Christmas necklace. I'd dusted gold glitter on my eyelids. Although I felt like an outsider, there was no way around it: for more than 380 days since The Accident, I'd been a member of this population.

I teared up as I peered in and watched these compromised people having such a jolly time in spite of their wheelchairs and mobility devices. I remembered what Taylor had said about the C.O.R.E. population. No one wants to be here. They're here by circumstance, not by choice. But tonight, we were all here by choice. I hadn't met many of the other clients because I'd been so closed-off and focused during my ninety-minute sessions that it was like I was wearing blinders. I wondered if any of the few people I'd met were here tonight.

Once, while Taylor was pounding on my heel and calf with a percussive device, a man with cool shoulder-length hair arrived. He drove himself to C.O.R.E. in a Rolls Royce he'd bought with proceeds from his lawsuit against the city of Santa Monica when a tree had fallen on him and left him paralyzed. And there were the Michaels—the three men who came in about the same time I did and were all named Michael, including that LAPD cop. One day, I was at the leg extension machine, and Taylor was comparing the strength of my right leg with my injured left leg. Directly in front of us, a much older woman was stooped over her walker, wearing huge, dark, hide-my-famous-face Hollywood sunglasses. I asked Taylor, "What's with the glasses?"

"Macular degeneration," he said. "She can't tolerate light." She was ninety-four and had been coming to C.O.R.E. for ten years.

And then there was the young woman, maybe eighteen max, younger than the average client. She'd been out hiking, missed a step, and had fallen down a cliff. Since her story rang so close for me—she had been hiking—I'd hung around and asked her a question. She had brushed me off, said she didn't want to talk about it. Since she hadn't been very friendly or sociable, I didn't expect to see the young hiker at the Christmas party.

I wiped away the tears, calmed my pre-party jitters, and went inside. The place smelled piney from the Christmas tree. A danceable version of "Jingle Bells" was playing, and I started to move with the upbeat music. I waved hi to Brittney, the manager, who looked especially pretty with her hair down for a change. The physical therapy tables had been shoved together with a white tablecloth on top. I added my fruit salad to the smorgasbord of good, home-cooked holiday foods—pulled pork, poached salmon, corn pudding. To ease myself into the party and give me something to do, I helped myself to the pulled pork. As I enjoyed some of the deliciously creamy mac and cheese, I looked around for a familiar face. Maybe one of the Michaels would be here.

A man wearing a seasonal red sweater said hi and introduced himself as Steve. He had a plate of food on his lap and was steadying a drink between his legs. Usually when you meet someone you make eye contact and shake hands, but with me standing at five-foot-eight and Steve down there in the wheelchair, the social connection felt awkward. If I knelt, would that be misunderstood?

I found Taylor sipping a cup of eggnog at the far side of the room, away from the music. "What's the etiquette when you're introduced to someone in a wheelchair?" I asked him.

In Malcolm Gladwell's book *Talking to Strangers*, he wrote that when we interact with people we don't know, we must make eye contact. I explained to Taylor that I'd failed at that with Steve. "Should I have knelt down in front of him, so Steve and I were eye to eye?"

"Good question," said Taylor, putting his plate aside for a moment. "People in wheelchairs are tired of looking at crotches and butts. They don't like the pity card either. Yes, kneeling is nice."

I made a mental note to put my new knowledge into action immediately: find Steve, kneel down, and talk to him, eye to eye. But since I still had Taylor's attention, and we were in a quiet area, I asked him something else I'd been curious about. Because so many of the clients at C.O.R.E. were men, young men, I wondered, did these poor guys never get to have sex again? Speaking for myself, I couldn't imagine life without another orgasm. Orgasms are the exclamations marks of my days.

Taylor rattled off the results of a survey involving spinal cord injury patients. "The first thing they want back is the function of their bowel and bladder, the second is sexual function, and then way down on the list is the ability to walk."

I stared at Taylor. "That's fascinating. They wanna have sex more than they wanna walk again?"

I looked at some of the men at the party—Michael, the injured cop who I'd watched struggling to walk, was here and wearing an ugly Christmas sweater with a bespectacled reindeer on the front. "From what I've read, some guys can still have sex. But it seems so sad."

The authors of *Enabling Romance: A Guide to Love, Sex, and Relationships for the Disabled* wrote that there are millions of people with disabilities who eventually discover they can enjoy sexual satisfaction despite their physical limitations.

"Spinal cord injury isn't a brain injury," said Taylor. "You still have the desire, but there's no connection between the brain and 'down there,' so it's very frustrating for blokes."

At our next session, I told Taylor, "That was the best party of the holiday season." I didn't mention the only thing that was missing was dancing. I hadn't been expecting tango time at C.O.R.E., but my mother had always said, "Never sit if you can dance." My mother's mantra didn't jibe with this population.

"When you rock up to a place and people want to be there, you can tell," said Taylor. "It's the British South African way. Don't strive for perfection but for connection."

CHAPTER 20

You've Come a Helluva Long Way

A freak accident—falling down the stairs at home—almost destroyed my ambulatory life. With approximately four thousand tendons in the human body, the rupture of the largest one, the Achilles, dislocated everything. Two years and six surgeries after The Accident, this one-Achillied woman walks at half the speed of others. Maybe she's resigned to the fact that this might be her new normal. The best new version of herself. But she still doesn't buy it. She isn't ready to settle, to accept that this is as good as it's going to be.

Ed reminds me that perfect is the enemy of good.

Dr. Kelli Harding, assistant clinical professor of psychiatry at Columbia University Medical Center, has observed that illness alone is not a predictor of outcome. She says it may boil down to this: Are you alone when you're sick, or do you have people sending you flowers and bringing you magazines? If you do, you're going to get better faster. Our interconnectedness helps us stay healthier.

I'm convinced that deep connections with my husband, family, neighbors, friends—especially those who dropped everything to visit me in the scary times—and the collective collaboration of the doctors on my Recovery Team, plus my own resilience and stubborn determination, helped me recover and walk again when others who are orthopedically challenged might not. Maria Popova, writer of a blog called *The Marginalian*, says, "Every loss reveals what we are made of."* Without realizing it, I grabbed hold of and redefined my prognosis instead of letting my prognosis define me.

Recently, a welder on a jobsite in our neighborhood commented, "You're walking better, right?" His observation caught me off guard. So, people I didn't even know, strangers, had been watching me walk on our street. I smiled back at the welder and paused to stand straighter, throwing my shoulders back, before I tottered off.

I try to smile at everyone I pass when I'm out walking in my neighborhood, and most people smile back, but I hadn't realized that they were also observing me. The first time I ventured out without my hiking poles, Brian, our mailman, asked, "No sticks?"

When Ed and I entered OLLO's, a local Malibu breakfast place, Luis, our favorite waiter, stopped as he was about to deliver a meal to another table. Used to seeing Scooter Girl, he said, "Wow! Look at you!" I paused and sputtered a reply because I was always taken aback when anyone out in public—Sam the dry cleaner, Cruz the grocery cashier, Luis the waiter—noticed my progress.

Although others might be praising my progress, I wanted *more.*

---

* Maria Popova, "Every Loss Reveals What We Are Made of: Blue Bananas, Why Leaves Change Color, and the Ongoing Mystery of Chlorophyll," *The Marginalian* blog, accessed March 5, 2025, https://www.themarginalian.org/2021/10/26/why-leaves-change-color/.

I texted Taylor while I was taking an afternoon walk: It's no longer step-*thump*. Now it's more step-*step*, but I'm going maddeningly slow. Everybody whizzes by. I'm still going at half-speed.

"To compare is the quickest way to despair," Taylor wrote back. "Instead, celebrate your daily efforts, your personal victories."

One day, Taylor, who was proud of my progress and who also knows Fred, said, "What do you think Fred would say if he saw you here now?"

"A normal person would say, 'Wow, it's been over a year and she's still pounding away at PT. That's sad.'" I paused. "But Fred's so macho, and the golden halo always surrounds him, so he'd probably say, 'Look how well she's doing. What happened wasn't that big of a deal.' But you know what I'd really like to do if I ever saw him?"

Taylor gave me a quizzical look.

"I've never hit anyone in my life. But I'd smack him." I paused. "The question is would I hit his face flat with my palm, or punch him with my fist?" The feeling of wanting to hit him scared me because it was so strong, and I'd never had that feeling of really wanting to physically injure someone.

Another way of punching the guy would've been to sue him for malpractice for my botched surgery. People who knew my story asked if I was going to sue the surgeon, and when I said no, they always asked, "Why not?" I'd never intended to sue the jerk because that would have been piling more negative energy onto an already negative situation. It's also been my experience that lawsuits are gnarly, and I was ready to move on to the positive, not linger in the negative.

After reading Atul Gawande's *Complications: A Surgeon's Notes on an Imperfect Science*, my reasons for not suing were confirmed. Gawande says mistakes are an inevitable part of medicine and mentions several surgical mishaps:

> *How could anyone who makes mistakes of that magnitude be allowed to practice medicine? We call such doctors "incompetent," "unethical," and "negligent." We want to see them punished. And so we've wound up with the public system we have for dealing with error: malpractice lawsuits, media scandal, suspensions, firings. There is, however, a central truth in medicine that complicates this tidy vision of misdeeds and misdoers: all doctors make terrible mistakes.*
>
> *The deeper problem with medical malpractice suits is that by demonizing errors they prevent doctors from acknowledging and discussing them publicly.*
>
> *When things go wrong, it is almost impossible for a physician to talk to a patient honestly about mistakes. Hospital lawyers warn doctors that although they must, of course, tell patients about injuries that occur, they are never to intimate that they were at fault, lest the "confession" wind up in court.**

Let's also not forget Fred was a world-famous hip doctor who

---

* Atul Gawande, *Complications: A Surgeon's Notes on an Imperfect Science* (New York:Picador, 2002).

worked on champion athletes, mostly basketball players. Every time there was another important game broadcast on TV, you'd see Fred down there on the court, center stage, just in case something happened. One doctor who had recently been at a medical conference told me Fred was so out of it that he probably introduced my infection during the surgery because he hadn't kept his operating theater clean enough. Even so, if anyone ever sued him for malpractice, I could see some of the other doctors and basketball players rushing to his defense.

Although my handicapped parking sticker was good for another three years, I no longer used it at C.O.R.E. I left those spots for people who needed it more.

At the end of our next session, Taylor said, "You get what you train for, and you keep what you train for. You've come a helluva long way, but the closer you get to your target, the harder it is. Want to see your walking video from when you first came here for a dose of inspiration?"

A data-driven optimist, Taylor compared the numbers. A year ago, I'd walked fourteen steps in 10.3 seconds in six meters. Today, I'd walked nine steps in 4.5 seconds in six meters.

"That's incredible!" he said. "Double the speed in half the time."

"You're happy with my progress."

"I'm not happy. I'm ecstatic."

The number of steps wasn't the only thing that was different. In the first video, as I walked the red rungs of the stepladder that were taped to the floor, I'd teetered from one end of the room to the other, off-balance, wobbly. Visibly slumpy, there was nothing cheerful or upbeat about my appearance or ambulation. For her first day at

C.O.R.E., the "don't be drab" girl had worn an old shirt and baggy sweatpants; those blah items reflected how sad and worn-out I had felt. I looked and walked like a has-been.

In the current video, the difference was so startling: it was as though we were looking at a different person. As Taylor said, "It's like watching those movies in black and white, and suddenly they pop into color."

I was wearing a flattering, tight-fitting, red-and-white-striped jersey that showed off my waist; black yoga pants; and a red Bauerfeind medical-grade orthopedic ankle brace over my left stocking, something my friend Linda had introduced me to. It's so small and lightweight you hardly notice it. Before I set off in my stocking feet from the far side of the room, I gave Taylor a robust cheerleader's wave to signal I was ready for him to begin taping. He gave me the go-ahead, and I charged across the room, my arms enthusiastically swinging in sync with my steps. I was walking, and walking faster. I was also stable, agile, smiling. Smiling. I was smiling! I looked like a new person.

John Gorospe, another therapist at C.O.R.E. who watched the "then" and "now" videos running side by side, said, "You've got some pep in your step now."

Next to John, Stephanie Mendoza, the former intern (now a therapist), said, "Your steps sound different."

Those two videos were a perfect illustration of how the body is a fully integrated unit. They showed clearly that when one part is off—in my case, a dead Achilles, but in someone else's case, something like cancer, diabetes, or heart disease—it throws off the whole body, inside and out, physically and psychologically.

Celebrating with Taylor at one of my last therapy days at C.O.R.E.

"I hope you feel very proud of yourself," Taylor said. "You had a mountain to climb. How many people do you know who tore their Achilles and it died? You had no point of reference, nothing. You were on your own. When people say, 'Hey, Jo, you're in the 1 percent of people who recover,' just correct them and say, 'Actually I'm in the .01 percent.' When you first came to see me, you said, 'I want to hike to waterfalls.' But it wasn't realistic."

"That's all very nice," I said. But I was still impatient. "What are my chances for a full recovery?"

Taylor got a piece of paper from Danea at the front desk, and with a thick felt-tip pen, he wrote in big, black letters:

I do the best I can with what I've been given based on how I'm feeling right now!

"Yes, I can see improvement." I hesitated because I suspected the hard truth was that walking, for me, would never be as carefree and easy as it once was. "I want to get better. I'm still favoring the right side."

"You're happy but definitely not satisfied," said Taylor. "It takes one thousand days, three years, to recover from an orthopedic injury. The start date is not from the date of injury but when you start PT and training."

"So, I have another year to go?"

"Yes, but you're a medical miracle. A testimonial to conquering your prognosis. People say it can't be done, but look at you. The number one predictor for recovery is attitude."

According to Taylor, there are three categories of clients at C.O.R.E. Category 1 are the High Achievers, the 5 percent who are doing everything they're supposed to be doing to maximize their success and recovery. They come on time; they're consistent. They'll do well. Category 2 are the Unfulfilled clients, the 70 percent who meet the minimal effective dose of restorative exercise but are not doing everything to maximize their success and optimize their recovery. Category 3 are the Underachievers, the 25 percent who don't want to be there. Their families and doctors insist they come.

Early on, Taylor had classified me as a High Achiever. He said I was consistent, compliant, and adherent to what I needed to do to obtain a winning outcome.

"And I had an excellent coach!" I said to him. Taylor's identical twin brother was a magician with an international reputation. He'd once gotten a whole group of us into Hollywood's Magic Castle. "And you're a magician, too," I said.

We exchanged fist bumps and with tears in my eyes, I said, "Thanks for caring so much." Taylor identifies as a restorative exercise therapist, and I told him he should change that to restorative *life* therapist.

"We all have to do what we don't want to do, to get to what we want to do." Taylor paused. "Enjoy hiking in Montana, getting back to the waterfalls." Then Taylor reminded me that one of C.O.R.E.'s slogans is, "Better has no finish line."

CHAPTER 21

A Waterfall Junkie's Wet Dream

Eight months after The Accident. We arrived back in Bozeman for the first time since this medical debacle began. As we were approaching the road up to our house, Denny, a neighbor, was down at the mailboxes.

"How are you doing?" asked Ed.

"I need knee surgery," he said. "I'm putting it off because of sepsis. What I've been through," he sighed.

I can't remember if I actually said it or just thought it: I've had six surgeries in less than six months. I win this competition.

It reminded me of the bereavement group I'd attended after my husband died. A person was attending the group because her roommate's hamster had died. The grief counselor had said, "Everyone's grief is the worst."

Maybe everyone's surgery is the worst, too.

I'd just started unpacking when Valerie phoned to say her husband was coming down the mountain with dinner. You know how some neighbors are irreplaceable? That's Val and Cam. Over the years they'd become our Welcoming Committee. (A few years later, Val and Cam would move off our mountain, mostly to avoid the long Montana winters with black ice on our road, and we'd be heartbroken.)

When I heard Cam pull up, I went out to greet him. Neighbors who are kind enough to make dinner and deliver it deserve a full welcome.

"You're walking!" said Cam, as he jumped down from his pickup.

"It's more like limping and lurching."

"I thought you'd be in a wheelchair or using a walker."

"It's an experiment this summer to see if I can manage without a left Achilles."

"But you can't walk without an Achilles," he said, repeating what most people think, doctors included.

I lifted the bottom of my pajama leg to show him the thick, disfiguring, brownish scar. Most friends were too squeamish to look at the nasty reminder of a medical situation gone bad. Once, I was about to show it to my strapping six-foot-five nephew and he looked the other way, wincing: "I don't like to see things like that."

After I brought Cam's lovely platter of warm roasted chicken inside, I went upstairs to get dressed. When Ed and I had first arrived back here, going up those seventeen stairs to our bedroom scared me to death. I was not sure I could do it. But we weren't going to sleep in the living room, right? Whether I was going up or down, I was afraid. I made extra-sure I planted my left foot down firmly. Every time. No breezing up and down stairs for me. Ever again. I paused between each step as I clung to the banister. For the rest of my life, I'd never go up or down these stairs, or any stairs, in a carefree manner.

After I changed out of my pajamas, I sat on our front porch and laced up my favorite red Oboz hiking boots, the same ones I'd worn to summit Storm Castle Peak with Brad and Ed one Fourth of July—five miles round trip, 7,165-foot elevation. Shelton Johnson said in *Gloryland* that all you need to get to heaven is a good pair of boots. My red suede Oboz are my boots to heaven. I grabbed my hiking poles, the ones with the bear bell attached. These are my favorite outdoor friends—boots, poles, sun hat—and it felt like home reconnecting with them. The challenge I'd given myself that morning was walking our rural driveway.

One summer, I made this walk every morning with a deer who waited on the front porch and accompanied me. I'd be inside making myself a cup of coffee in the kitchen, and this fully grown deer would peer in through the glass window next to the front door, cocking her head—what's taking you so long? I'd come out in my robe with my hot coffee, and then the most amazing thing would happen: This white-tailed doe with warm, brown fur, her tiny ears fully alert, pointed up and back, would trot along on my left side, her doe eyes on me. A Bambi moment. She walked so close that I could smell her musky scent. She and I did this extraordinary walk down our driveway and back—woman and deer duet—every morning that summer. I don't know what was in it for her. I never gave her any treats. Although sometimes I'd catch her and her siblings nibbling on our flowers—snapdragons, peonies—they weren't seriously interested in our mostly deer-resistant garden. By the end of summer, I was tempted to reach out and pet my morning walking pal. Friends advised: "Don't you dare. They have skin diseases." Years later when I'd do this morning driveway walk alone, I'd miss the company of my deer, and I'd marvel in amazement at the pure magic that our crazy, unlikely duet had ever happened and, sadly, would probably never happen again. My loss.

After Cam's dinner was safely inside, I kissed Eddie goodbye, and step by test step, I started off from our front porch. As I said, my goal was to attempt to walk our rural driveway. It's a pretty low goal—just walking the driveway—but it loomed large. I gripped the cork handles of my poles, jabbed the tips into the asphalt of our driveway, and put my best foot forward.

Next to the garage, the stand of aspens quaking in the wind had already turned impossibly green. With all the rain, the world up here was so lush you could lick it. And smell it. The lawn had recently been mowed, perfuming the mountain air.

Step after shaky step, I slowly, carefully made it to our rickety fence—seventy-one steps.

A scattering of the tiniest bluebirds fluttered out of the little wooden bird houses attached to the fence, many more birds than usual. Dozens spiraled up into the sunlight, iridescent turquoise shimmering on the underside of their wings. This was a take-away-your-breath spectacle, and it was right on our driveway. I wish Ed had seen it. A squirrel scurried into the smoky gray chaparral. I rested on my hiking poles as I stopped to watch the amusing family of plump grouse that had taken up residence at our place. They paraded single file across the driveway right in front of me.

Step by cautious step, I made it to the first curve.

One hundred and twenty-two steps.

The slow, small steps were adding up. Cautiously, I made it to the Little Bear Ranch sign, which you know is a joke.

One hundred and fifty-three steps.

I paused along the fence line again, and then finally reached my goal: all the way to the end of our driveway.

Five hundred and twenty-five steps.

I made it!

In my previous life, pre-Accident, I would always turn left onto the dirt road and breeze up to the top of the mountain—6,500 steps up and back—and I figured they counted for more at altitude, elevation 6,180 feet at the top.

Walking our driveway loomed like an impossible first goal.

Managing to successfully "hike" our driveway—1,050 steps round trip—left me feeling radiant, and had given me enough confidence that I wanted to try Hyalite. A few miles south of Bozeman, Hyalite is a popular hike—only 2.6 miles round trip—to a favorite waterfall.

Through all those agonizing months trapped in bed with my leg elevated in a cast, while having to rely on that knee scooter, the image that was front and center in my mind like a visual mantra was the entry path at Hyalite to Grotto Falls. As a self-described waterfall junkie, my wet dream has always been hiking to a waterfall, and it doesn't have to be the biggest or the longest, just a waterfall, the grace of water falling. So it was curious that the image this waterfall junkie turned to for comfort in the darkest times had been the path to the waterfall, not the falls.

Visualizing that wide, green entry path was my calm-down image when I started hyperventilating and could not stand being locked in that hyperbaric oxygen chamber one more second. That entry is an invitation to a green world of a half-million roadless acres, and it was my escape hatch, the place I mentally took myself when I didn't know if I'd walk again, let alone hike on that forest path. Lana had asked during that dark period, "Do you think of yourself as an *ex-hiker*?" No, never! When we have guests who aren't outdoorsy—New Yorkers who self-describe as sidewalk walkers—we bring them to Hyalite because it's an easy, pleasant forest stroll rather than a hard hike.

When Ed and I pulled into the parking lot at the Hyalite Creek Trail on Sunday morning, there weren't many cars. Some people go to church on Sundays; some go hiking. As a friend had just texted, "Hiking's my favorite Sunday Service." An official BE BEAR AWARE sign next to the outhouse reminded people, as if they needed it, that this is bear country and to carry bear spray. I prefer this remote area when it's more populated, and in our excitement of getting to Hyalite, we'd forgotten our bear spray. We had backups—bear bells on our poles that jingled as we walked, and a bear whistle dangling on a cord around my neck. That yellow plastic whistle looked dinky, but its fierce, piercing sound could be heard from blocks away.

It was a brisk Montana July morning—about forty-five degrees. A Chamber of Commerce Montana summer day. While inhaling the clean forest aroma, we bundled up: Ed had two layers over his fishing shirt; on top of my hiking shirt, I zipped on a red puffy vest, added a lumberjack flannel shirt, and strapped on a fanny pack with a thermos of water for us.

With no bear spray, maybe I should have been fearful, but I wasn't. I would never have turned around and driven another forty-five minutes on that dusty, bumpy, unpaved road back into town for bear spray. Once, when we were on the rugged Spanish Creek trail in the Lee Metcalf Wilderness, we saw three bears off the trail just to the left of us, about fifty feet away, though as you can imagine, they felt closer. After we clustered with the other hikers on the trail, one of whom had a gun but not a bear rifle, the bears went their way and we went ours. Except for the adrenaline rush, it was no big deal. Or maybe we were getting used to coexisting with bears.

The trail at Hyalite is not a narrow trail hemmed in by sly, high grasses. Instead, it's wide and welcoming and bordered by sentinels of hundred-foot lodgepole pines. Even though I felt creaky and stiff after not being on a trail for over seven months, my footfalls on the soft forest floor were steady, quiet. After the first few steps, I'd expected to feel something *more*. Something instantly celebratory.

Maybe a band would be playing. Confetti. Air horns. I was doing it! I was hiking Hyalite!

My first hike after losing my left Achilles.

Just beyond the wide-open meadow sprinkled with alpine wildflowers and lacey yarrows, I plopped down on a mossy cushion in the forest shade. This forest is so dense that the big sky is mostly hidden by leafy canopies. The trail smelled minty green—like fresh spearmint, as strong as if I'd chopped a handful for Ed for mint juleps on Derby Day. Since I'd never smelled mint on this trail, I kept sniffing, searching for the source of the sweet aroma. There was an eerie mountain stillness as I blew on my cold fingertips. We should've remembered gloves, but who thinks of gloves in summer?

Resting on that mossy tree trunk, I hadn't collapsed. I wasn't tired. My ankle wasn't killing me. I was smiling, taking a break to savor the feeling: I'd walked 1,400 steps. I had made it to the meadow! Being able to walk on this path had loomed like such a quest. Now that I was here, it seemed like everything and nothing: I was doing it—walking the path to Grotto Falls at Hyalite. This simplest pleasure—Walking in Nature—being able to ambulate and being able to do it in a forest made me happy, beyond happy. After the long slog of rehabbing my ankle, I was starting to feel whole again.

Ed and I weren't charging straight to the waterfall like we usually do. Instead, I was present right there on the soft bark path, savoring every footfall. The bear bell on my hiking pole clanked the whole time, as it should.

Each time I dawdled, resting on a boulder, a tree trunk, a fallen log, sitting under a cathedral of trees, inhaling cool gulps of the sweet evergreen air, I was puzzled: why am I sitting again? Was it that at 6,920 feet altitude I needed to catch my breath? No. Was the gentle uphill grade—an elevation gain of only 250 feet—too much? No. I was savoring the thrill that I was suddenly on this wonderful hiking path, walking to a favorite waterfall.

As I reached out, stroking the rough bark of a lodgepole pine, I was reminded of my friend, Luchita, an artist. "Trees are my relatives," she had said. No wonder Luchita was my heart-mate.

Seeing me sitting again, Ed circled back. Everyone has their own natural pace, and he couldn't walk as slowly as I was walking. Although he has that tricky right ankle, he's compensated for it since childhood. "We don't have to go all the way this first time," he said.

"I can do it!" I tightened the upper laces on my boots, took off my jacket, tied it around my waist, grabbed the poles, and started off.

Don't get me wrong. I wasn't "walking" like the able-bodied person I used to be. Now I placed my good foot down to stabilize myself, and then I'd take the quickest, littlest baby step with my "involved" foot (as Taylor called it), and pivot back *fast* onto my good foot. Since we all compensate toward the side of strength, my good right leg was still *over-compensating* for my limp left leg.

When families rushed by, I'd remind myself what Taylor had said, "To compare is to despair."

With Hyalite Creek gently burbling alongside, we made the turn at the fork, glimpsed the old granite landslide, passed the lone picnic table, and knew we were closing in on the falls. I'd been listening for the first roar of water, and finally heard the full force of water thundering. Everyone in town had been talking about the big spring melt-off, and how the waterfalls were running fuller and more powerfully than usual. Then we saw it. With a fifty-foot drop and about twenty feet wide, Grotto Falls isn't the longest, widest, or splashiest waterfall, but it's wonderful!

This is a wild green place with nothing commercial, no snack bar, no souvenir shop with postcards, no restroom. Recently someone—the Parks Service?—had thoughtfully carved steps into the muddy bank, so you no longer slip and slide getting to the splashdown. Balancing on my hiking poles on the slick, wet stones next to the river bottom, I felt the vibration, the cool mist with its helpful negative ions. I inhaled deep breaths of the super-oxygenated cascading water and felt myself happily filling with super-oxygenated energy. My brain on waterfall. As you know by now, for me, waterfalls are magic—they release a happy feeling. My body vibrated. I could have lingered and returned the next day for more.

With the soundtrack of Mother Nature cascading in front of us, I was reminded of a John Muir quote:

To sit in solitude.
To think in solitude.
With only the music
Of the stream and the cedar
to break the flow of silence,
there lies the value of wilderness.

I peeled off another layer and was down to my red-and-white plaid Patagonia hiking shirt when Ed snapped a photo of me balancing at the edge of the creek in front of the powerfully cascading water, poles raised high in the air. My *Rocky* moment.

I sent the photo to everyone. I did it! As Henry David Thoreau said, "I took a walk in the woods and came out taller than the trees."

My *Rocky* moment!

CHAPTER 22

Congratulations! You're a Local Hero!

I'm not comfortable with the phrase "medical miracle," but *The Argonaut*, a local Los Angeles paper, did a cover story on me entitled "Defying an Achilles Heel," and that's what the writer called me: a medical miracle.

Then five years after The Accident, in winter 2024, out of the blue I received a joyous message from someone named Paige King at Oboz Footwear that was about, well, me. For at least a dozen years, probably more, I'd been wearing my favorite red suede Oboz boots when I hike. This high-performance hiking shoe has the best traction. It hugs my narrow foot like no other, and even in the riskiest situations—think of that waterfall with Brad in the Crazies—it makes every single step safe and secure. Since red is my favorite color, choosing their Rio red suede boot was a no-brainer.

Here's what Paige's email said:

> *Congratulations, Jo. It's time to celebrate you because you are one of Oboz's 6 Local Heroes for 2024!*

I was surprised and flattered. How often in everyday life are any of us singled out and celebrated as a hero?

What is a Local Hero anyway, I wondered. Paige King, marketing and community coordinator at Oboz Footwear, explained:

> *When it comes to the path ahead, you can go their way. The line of least resistance. Or you can pick a path less traveled in exchange for bettering yourself and more importantly, your community. This is what we call a Local Hero. A world that's up to us to nurture, explore, revere and celebrate. A pursuit defined by the compass in our hearts, the miles beneath our feet and the rules that have yet to be written. Whether the trail involves defending the places we traverse or stoking the adventures we can't quit, our community shines brighter thanks to hard-charging people like you who pave the way forward.*

Of the six 2024 Local Heroes, two were Montanans, two were in Colorado, one was a New Hampshire native, and another lived in Pennsylvania.

I was pleased, but I felt compelled to ask Paige, "Why me? Why am I being honored?"

I wasn't asking to be flattered. I was curious.

She said, "You were selected for your inspiring story of perseverance and *GRIT*. Overcoming an injury and coming out stronger than ever."

She sent me the note my nominator, Dr. Taylor Isaacs, had submitted:

> *A hiker since she was five, Jo ruptured her left Achilles in a freak accident and lost it after a botched surgery. Her chances of walking and hiking again were slim. For 2.5 years she showed an unwavering dedication to a restorative exercise regimen. Her commitment allowed her to overcome the life-challenging aftermath of her Achilles tendon dying. As the Kinesiologist/Restorative Exercise Specialist who worked with her, I told her, when people say, "Hey, Jo, you're in the 1 percent of people who recover, just correct them and say, "Actually I'm in the .01 percent." She emerged triumphant and as a self-described waterfall junkie she has returned to hiking to her favorite waterfalls, especially Hyalite, Ousel, and Big Timber Falls in the Crazies.*

The Oboz company, which is coincidentally headquartered in Bozeman, got its name by combining Outside + Bozeman = Oboz. The company says that right outside their front door, the mountains beckon them. Me, too.

Paige connected me with Kenny Gamblin, their photographer. "We'd love for him to capture some images of you out there doing what you do best." Since Kenny had already decided he wanted to shoot me hiking to a local waterfall, and because the road to Hyalite was closed until May and he needed to shoot in April, he selected Ousel Falls in Big Sky.

I know Ousel well. Remember that wonderful winter hike Lana and I did on New Years Day when the trail was all sparkling white with snow and ice? I've hiked it in winter wearing those helpful Yaktrax with spikes, and in summer in my Oboz boots. But I'd never been there in late April, so I was concerned, not knowing what to expect. It could be snowing with a white-out. Not good for photographer or hiker. If it had recently been raining, the trail could be muddy and slippery. And if the snow had started melting, there could be leftover patches where the steep downhill sections might be icy-slick.

Kenny checked and rechecked weather predictions and upped the day of our shoot because of the iffy weather. He and Paige agreed that frozen waterfalls could be fine, because as Paige said, "It could be framed around the idea of Jo still getting out and doing her favorite thing despite the season."

After Kenny rescheduled our shoot multiple times, I met him in late April outside the Oboz headquarters in downtown Bozeman, along with his assistant, Elsa Tritsch, a Montana State University student. He looked over the footwear I'd lined up in the trunk of my car and selected my older, well-worn red Oboz boots, and the HOKAs with the Yaktrax, just in case there was ice. Since Kenny didn't want to shoot in flat midday sun, we left in time to catch the glow of the more flattering golden-hour, late-afternoon light.

An hour later when we arrived at Ousel, it was forty-eight degrees, with the sun trying to poke through the puffy white clouds, and a slight breeze. Since the next day was predicted to be twenty-eight degrees and snowing, Kenny had made the right decision to shoot today.

After we parked at Ousel, and after I used the smelly porta-potty, I walked over to the trailhead to check out the surface. "It's perfect!"

I called back to Kenny and Elsa. "It's dirt, dry dirt. No ice or snow in sight." Of course, I'd only glanced at the uppermost part of the trail. Instead of Yaktrax, I reached for my hiking boots.

"You could put the Yaktrax on the boots," Kenny suggested, concern in his voice.

"I don't think they'd fit," I said. Besides, how in the world could I stretch those ornery Yaktrax over that thick sole. "I don't need them. Up here, it's dry dirt." Famous last words.

Kenny crammed his photography equipment into a bulky backpack, and Elsa carried a reflector for him, and an extra jacket for me in case it got colder. I pocketed a tube of red lipstick, and since I wasn't sure if the bears were out of hibernation, I fastened bear bells to my hiking poles. Then the three of us set off happily on our photo adventure to the waterfall.

Down at the first curve, there were leftover patches of icy snow near the picnic table, but I wasn't overly concerned because there was also some dirt on the shoulder of the trail, so we could inch along over there if we needed to.

The familiar old wooden bridge, about a hundred feet long, eight feet across, was as dry and walkable as in summer. Kenny directed me to cross the bridge dozens of times while he shot from many angles. My confidence in this photographer grew as he didn't settle for one shot but kept directing me for different views. I didn't feel self-conscious because I was wearing my comfortable, old outdoor clothes—brown Patagonia hiking pants and shirt, red vest—and I was in my element, out in nature, bear bells ringing, doing what I love best.

Me being photographed as a Local Hero.

This was five years after The Accident. Who would've thought just a few years ago, when I hadn't walked for 144 days and had all those surgeries, that I'd be out here, able to do this again?

After snapping many shots, we moved to the first uphill curve where the shade had blanketed the slope in black ice. I dug my poles in and stopped to scan the trail for safety. Kenny went ahead, shooting back at me, and since the trail had also been trampled by previous hikers, I used their footprints as a guide for where it was safe to step.

About halfway to the falls, this icy trail was so demanding, with too many scary patches, that I paused. Usually a hiking trail speaks to me lovingly, but it felt like this trail was telling me to call it quits and turn back. I didn't mention this to my hiking buddies because they had a job to do, and we'd driven all this way. And I'd never ever turned around on a hike. I sucked it up and plunged ahead.

Deep in the forest was the first clear straightaway where tall evergreen trees loomed on both sides of the trail. When we stopped at another picnic table, I told Kenny how my friend Lana and I had ended up here one New Years Day. I motioned toward the hundred-foot-wide rocky wall directly in front of us. "In January, that was all turquoise ice," I said. Now in April, that huge wall had just one measly leftover blob of melting ice.

Along the way, Kenny and Elsa, both athletes and rock climbers, compared their ages. Elsa was twenty, Kenny thirty. I'm usually not one to flaunt my age freely, but after listening to them and feeling so in my element, I piped up, "I'm seventy-seven."

"No!" said Elsa. "I thought you were in your fifties, max."

Maybe Nature is the best anti-aging tonic.

While he was driving, Kenny had also asked about my injury, and when I told him I had no left Achilles, he was shocked. "No!" he said. "That's not possible. You can't walk without an Achilles."

More trail, more turns, another bridge, and finally this one-Achillied person made it to Ousel Falls. The robust spring runoff and the melting snow made this fifty-foot waterfall even louder and more powerful. Kenny had a choice of two levels to shoot from: the upper-view deck where we were, or way down at the bottom of the stairs at the splashdown. He seemed satisfied shooting from the upper view. For some reason, this super-athletic guy, a rock climber, who on our way to Ousel had pointed out the faces of steep mountains he'd climbed, seemed reluctant to venture to the splashdown. But I could see that the stairs were mostly clear of snow and ice, so I said, "Let's go down. We'll get better pictures down there." So far, I'd had a "good hair" day, but I told Kenny, "The mist from the waterfall will do this hair in."

Grabbing my hiking poles in one hand, and holding securely onto the cold, damp, metal handrail with the other, I super-cautiously and super-slowly started down the first of two nearly vertical flights of stairs. The flat, rocky surface next to the splashdown was covered in demonic black ice. It's no overstatement to say that one misstep, and someone could lose their footing and be swept away in the rushing current. Maybe I should've figured out a way to wear the Yaktrax after all.

Shooting from the shoreline, Kenny snapped some shots and proudly showed me what he'd gotten: close-ups of my face where the background was a blurry waterfall.

I wasn't happy with it. Too much me, not enough waterfall. I suggested we needed to see the entire waterfall in the background. Kenny sent Elsa back up the stairs for his wide-angle lens.

Standing out there balancing on the slippery black ice was the most daring thing I'd done since losing my Achilles. I couldn't help remembering that PT person who said to me, "You have to accept that you'll be compromised for the rest of your life." If only she could see me now.

Down there, as I stood with one foot on that iffy patch of ice and the other perched securely on a dry spot, Kenny shot the picture of the day.

"Now *that's* the heroic shot!" he said.

The heroic shot.

Epilogue

Recently, I showed up for a sunrise hike sponsored by Oboz Footwear. On October 3, 2024, we met at the Drinking Horse Trail, a favorite, easy 2.2-mile hike. As the thirty or so of us, bundled in extra layers because of the thirty-degree morning, sipped hot coffee and huddled around the pots of fire for warmth, I realized I'd never done a sunrise hike.

It's usually my style to be with the leader at the front of a hiking group. I like helping set the pace, and there's also less dust in your face when you're at the lead. But at 7:30 as the group hit the trail onto the forested path, I lagged behind. At the old wooden pedestrian bridge, I joined up with a guy whose company had just sent him to Taiwan. He said that from his hotel room in Taipei, he could open his door, step out, and hike up a mountain.

Because Ed and I had been talking about visiting Taiwan before the Chinese snatched it back, I enjoyed his story. But I was struggling to keep up. We were the stragglers, the very last ones in the group. I could not go faster.

As we rounded another curve and swatted the bushes out of our way, I said to him, "You go ahead."

He looked at me, concerned.

"No, no, it's fine," I motioned to him with my gloved hand. "Go ahead."

As I wandered back to the trailhead by myself, I also realized that since my accident and recovery, I'd mostly walked or hiked with one other person. Always someone like Roya, my Persian friend, who understood my pace. Or Connie, a new friend, who headed the Walkie-Talkies, a group in Bozeman who walk slow enough to chat.

On the drive home, hours earlier than I expected, the fact that I could no longer bomb up a mountain with an energetic group struck as a hard, sad realization.

The other day, I met a new colleague for the first time over coffee. I approached her feeling positive and curious about this interesting new person. At her table, this stranger who didn't know my story said, "You're limping."

Limping.

An arrow to the heart. I felt stricken and didn't know what to say. Limping. Still limping. Should I tell her I was just glad I was ambulating in whatever form?

Afterward when I told Ed, he said, "Well, you do plod."

Plod.

To compare is to despair. Revel in what I can do, and let language like limping and plodding fall by the wayside.

I had to bail on the sunrise hike. It was too fast for this one-Achillied woman.

Hiker's Logbook and Tips

Date: Record the date of your hike.

Location and trail name: City, State, Country

Trail: Is it hard, soft, slick, icy? How does it *feel*?

The Landscape, the vegetation: What does it *look* like?

The trees: Can you identify them?

Smell: Sniff the air. How does it *smell*?

Listen: What do you *hear*?

Touch: Touch a tree, a leaf. Is it smooth, rough, prickly?

Enjoyment: How much did you like or dislike the experience?

Difficulty: On a scale of one to ten, how easy or difficult was the hike?

Elevation Gain/Altitude: Record your elevation gain/altitude.

Steps: Keep track of how many steps you did.

Hiking buddies: Do not go alone. Safety tips for hiking by yourself are often offered, but basically it is not safe. Join a hiking group. Or get yourself a buddy.

Weather: Check the weather forecast before you head out. Pay attention to the winds, the heat, the chill. Walk in different weather—rain, snow, ice, sunshine, clouds, wind. But whatever weather you hike in, be safe.

Water: Bring extra. I bring mine in a Yeti container that I slip into a fanny pack, and it keeps the water icy cold.

Food: Small, lightweight snacks that you can stuff into your pack.

Clothes: Wear layers, and consider sunproof clothing from companies like Solumbra. If you'll be in areas with high grasses or bugs, wear long pants.

Boots: Do *not* wear street shoes with no traction. Oboz hiking boots don't need to be broken in, but some boots do. Break them in before you wear them on a hike. Hiking boots that fit properly should stabilize your feet and reduce the chance of blisters. In icy conditions, Yaktrax, the cleats that you fasten on the bottom of your shoes, are a must.

Sun protection: Sunscreen, sun hat, sunglasses.

Gear: Hiking poles and a backpack or fanny pack. If you're in bear country, bear protection—bear spray, whistle, and bear bells for your hiking poles.

Unplug: Keep your devices off. You can't engage your senses when you're plugged in.

Singing: Try singing as you hike. Whether you're feeling high or low, singing produces feel-good endorphins.

Be friendly: Make eye contact; greet other hikers with a smile and a friendly hello as you pass. This is also a chance to get current information on trail conditions.

Photo: Take a photo of yourself in front of a waterfall and share it. It could also be fun to check out waterfallswest.com for waterfalls near you that you might not know about!

National Park Service Etiquette Tips

- Hikers going uphill have the right of way
- Hikers going downhill, step aside, and give space to people hiking up
- Bicyclists yield to hikers—though they don't always do this, especially when they're speeding downhill
- Hikers yield to horses
- Stay on the trail

Acknowledgments

This book would not exist except for Joshua Mohr. I'd written what I thought was a personal essay about my Achilles journey. Except it was too long and I needed an editor to help me whip my forty-page document into the kind of short personal essay I was known for.

Author Samantha Dunn introduced me to Josh, who read my work and said, "This is spectacular! And it's not an essay. It's the map for a book."

A book.

Then Joseph Durepos, the literary agent, hopped on board, and said, "This is strong." Since he and his wife, Mary, are also hikers, we had fun working together. While he was heroically pitching the book, he'd send me pictures of their hikes around the Chicago area, and I'd send him pictures of mine, mostly in Montana and California.

I wouldn't have been able to navigate all the new publishing technology without Johnnie Tangle, my IT person. Johnnie had the patience of a saint, and no question of mine seemed too stupid or silly. Or, at least, Johnnie never let on. Thank you, Johnnie, for always being so polite, available, and helpful.

Myles Schrag, a total professional at Amplify Publishing, led me through the publishing process and made it easy and seamless. Myles was a joy to work with. And the art department at Amplify took a hard subject—a botched surgery and not walking—and made it lighter, more bearable for the reader by adding pops of color to the text.

I'm indebted to Taylor Isaacs. Not only is Taylor responsible for my walking again, he unintentionally gave the book its title. Taylor used to be a professional soccer player, and I was watching his video of the Liverpool soccer team where 60,000 fans were belting out the Liverpool fight song—*You'll Never Walk Alone!*—at the top of their lungs. It gave me chills, and immediately I knew that was the title.

I received so much support from so many, as any reader who has gotten this far in the book knows. I'm beyond grateful to all of you—and you know who you are, whether you're in the hiking world, the medical profession, or one of the dozens of friends, family, and neighbors who made my day when the days loomed dark. Thank you, kiitos, gracias.

And, first and foremost, huge hugs and kisses to my husband—Ed, Big E, Eddie—my lover, partner, best friend. He held my hand and walked alongside whether I was on crutches, in a wheelchair, or on that knee scooter. When I turned our story into *You'll Never Walk Alone*, he remained my biggest cheerleader.

About the Author

Jo Giese is an award-winning radio journalist, bestselling author of *Never Sit If You Can Dance: Lessons from My Mother*, teacher, community activist, former TV reporter at at WNBC-TV, and above all—an intrepid and enthusiastic hiker and world traveler.

As a special correspondent, she was part of a Peabody Award–winning team at *Marketplace*, the most popular business radio program in America. For those radio stories, Giese won an EMMA award for Exceptional Radio Story from the National Political Women's Caucus and a GRACIE Award from the Alliance for Women in Media.

Giese was featured on the cover of *The Argonaut* in November 2021, and in May 2024, she was honored as a Local Hero by Oboz

Footwear. She was a finalist in the Ultimate Explorer competition, which grants donations to the National Park Foundation.

She has visited more than fifty countries and hiked to over forty magnificent waterfalls in ten countries. Some of her favorites are Snoqualmie Falls (near Seattle), Halfmoon Falls (Big Timber, Montana), and Seljalandsfoss (Iceland). An alumna of the University of Texas at Austin, she has established the Jo Giese Excellence Endowment to assist other American Studies students.

She lives in Southern California and Bozeman, Montana, with her husband.

jogiese.com
@giesejo